Why We Fight

Also by Pandit Rajmani Tigunait

b o o k s

The Himalayan Masters: A Living Tradition
Inner Quest: The Path of Spiritual Unfoldment
At the Eleventh Hour: The Biography of Swami Rama
Tantra Unveiled: Seducing the Forces of Matter and Spirit
Swami Rama of the Himalayas: His Life and Mission
Shakti: The Power in Tantra (A Scholarly Approach)
From Death to Birth: Understanding Karma and Reincarnation
The Power of Mantra and the Mystery of Initiation
Shakti Sadhana: Steps to Samadhi
  (A Translation of the Tripura Rahasya)
Seven Systems of Indian Philosophy

a u d i o & v i d e o

The Spirit of the Upanishads
The Spirit of the Vedas
Pulsation of the Maha Kumbha Mela
In the Footsteps of the Sages
Living Tantra™ Series:
  Tantric Traditions and Techniques
  The Secret of Tantric Rituals
  Forbidden Tantra
  Tantra and Kundalini
  Sri Chakra: The Highest Tantric Practice
  Sri Vidya: The Embodiment of Tantra
Eight Steps to Self-Transformation
Nine Steps to Disarming the Mind

Why We Fight

practices for lasting peace

PANDIT RAJMANI TIGUNAIT

HIMALAYAN INSTITUTE
PRESS
HONESDALE, PENNSYLVANIA, USA

Himalayan Institute Press
RR 1 Box 1129
Honesdale, Pennsylvania 18431
www.HimalayanInstitute.org

Originally published as *Yoga on War & Peace*
© 1991, 2003 by The Himalayan International Institute of Yoga Science
and Philosophy of the USA.

Second edition 2003. First printing

Creative direction and cover design by Jeanette Robertson
Electronic design and production by Julia A. Valenza
Cover photos: Thermonuclear explosion: © Robert Marien/Index Stock;
flower: © Michel Frossard/Alamy. Inside image: Flying dove: © Andy Sotiriou /
Getty Images

The paper used in this publication meets the minimum requirements of
American National Standard for Information Sciences—Permanence of
Paper for Printed Library Materials, ANSI Z39.48-1984.

ISBN 0-89389-235-1

Dedicated to the peacemakers of all traditions
and to the sacred link connecting all human hearts.

contents

Ours is a violent world. War, insurrection, border incursions, mutiny, assassination, and just plain murder are woven into the fabric of human life. It's always been bad, and it's getting worse. According to the Peace Pledge Union, there have been more than 480 wars since 1700, resulting in more than 120 million deaths. And almost all of these people—95 percent—were killed in the twentieth century. How many is that? Estimates range from 115 to 140 million. That's an enormous range to be sure—25 million lives—but oddly enough, in an era awash with statistics, precise casuality figures are impossible to come by. There's no official agency charged with keeping a running body count, and the pitfalls of relying on information from parties to the slaughter are obvious.

Absolute numbers don't matter much anyway. Huge casualty figures numb the mind. We can comprehend the horror of a nightclub fire that kills 97, or (just barely) the attack on the World Trade Center with 2,863 dead, but figures in the hundreds of thousands—not to mention the millions—aren't human lives anymore, they're just statistics.

Organizations concerned with tracking war define an armed conflict as fighting that leaves a minimum cumulative total of 1,000 people dead. Sit for a moment and imagine the anguish that the loss of the two people nearest you would wreak in your life and the lives of those who depend on them. Take it all in and then multiply the wreckage by 500 (500! already the imagination wobbles) and you have a measure of the devastation caused by the smallest of the world's ongoing armed conflicts. In December of 1999, there were forty such conflicts raging in thirty-one different countries.

So here we are, looking over our shoulder at a century with a body count well above 100 million and no reason to believe that the numbers will do anything but rise—millions upon millions of lives snuffed out because we have never discovered how to manage our affairs without recourse to arms. This has got to change. The world is growing smaller and our weapons are becoming more potent (and more portable). It's way past time to get serious about extricating ourselves from the carnage.

In one sense, it's a simple matter. The saints and sages of all the great traditions tell us that war has its roots in a massive case of mistaken identity. "There's nothing to fight about and no one to fight with," they tell us. "We are all one. All things, all people are made from one essence and destined for one aim."

And what is that aim? Page through the last section of this book and listen to the voices echoing down the centuries and across cultures—saints and sages, rabbis, priests, imams, ministers, sadhus, and lay women and men from all traditions. "The phrase 'each other' doesn't make any sense," a thirteenth century Sufi poet proclaims. Or, in the words of a contemporary Buddhist, "When we look into our hearts and begin to discover what is confused and what is brilliant, what is bitter and what is sweet, it isn't just ourselves that we are discovering. We're discovering the universe." Einstein put it another way, "A human being is part of the whole, called by us 'universe,' a part limited by time and space. He experiences himself, his thoughts and feelings, as something separate from the rest—a kind of optical delusion of consciousness." The sage of the *Mundaka Upanishad* put it more simply, "The Lord is one light shining forth from every creature."

The aim we are all destined for is to know ourselves as that light. And when we do, violence vanishes. In the words of a Sioux holy man, "Peace comes within the souls of men when they realize their relationship, their oneness, with the Universe and all its powers."

There's a part of all of us that knows this is true. So why do we struggle so hard to hold ourselves separate? To assert "my" identity as apart from "your" identity, to make sure your rights aren't diminishing mine? Why are we so quick to feel threatened when your understanding of God differs from mine? The answers are the subject of the chapters that follow. But the author—a yoga master who has spent a lifetime helping people from all cultures overcome the obstacles to self-transformation—is offering us more than an inspiring explanation of why we fight and how we can stop. If inspiration alone were enough, the violence would have ended long ago. How much eloquence has been poured into pleas for peace? Over how many centuries? How many committed, impassioned people have devoted their lives to ending war? Yet the fighting goes on.

Lasting peace bubbles up from the same wellspring that feeds war—the depths of the human heart. That is the message of all of the world's great spiritual traditions. Here in these pages Pandit Tigunait offers us a series of practices—universal in appeal and application—for shedding our mistaken identity. When that drops away, when we know ourselves as light, we will find ourselves, in the words of Swami Rama, "to be part of the universe, and the universe to be part of us." And in that knowledge lies the seed of true and lasting peace.

Deborah Willoughby
Editor, *Yoga International*

Five great enemies to peace live within us: avarice,

ambition, envy, anger, and pride. If those enemies were

banished, we should infallibly enjoy perpetual peace.

—Petrarch

THE PRE-WAR CRISIS

WHY DO WE FIGHT?

No one likes war, yet war is perennial. We know the value of peace, yet we are restless without some unrest. Just as we, as individuals, are burdened with a variety of destructive habits, at the collective level we are burdened by wars, riots, political upheavals, and religious crusades. Yet, each time we fight, we pay a heavy price. The victors often lose more than those who suffer defeat on the battlefield.

Before a war breaks out, each side loudly proclaims its own righteousness and the opponent's wickedness. The populace vilifies the "enemy." Emotions are inflamed, war fever takes over, and little energy remains for finding a nonviolent solution to the conflict. Before the war begins, both parties claim that they are messengers of peace; sometimes the leaders even claim to be prophets or saviors.

Anyone with common sense knows this is true—we say we want peace, yet we wage war. By the time a war has run its course,

everyone is sickened by the slaughter, the torn and blackened land-
scape, the ruined cities, and the shattered lives. Survivors from both
sides—winners and losers, civilians and soldiers, leaders and citi-
zens vow never to go to war again. But alas, human memory is
short. Forgetting the lessons of the past, and failing to understand
the reasons that we fight, we soon find ourselves embroiled in yet
another conflict.

Several millennia ago, the sages of the yoga tradition pondered
these matters and concluded that the causes of such man-made
catastrophes are more subtle than we usually think. In the past,
gold, gems, land, religious beliefs, and women were the overt reasons for war. In modern times, women are no longer given as an
excuse, but the other elements remain unchanged.

According to yoga, stopping the cycle of war requires delving
into the subtle causes underlying the surface motives of material
gain and religious differences. These are selfishness, ego, greed, eth-
nocentrism, and sense of inferiority. Because of these, we fail to do
what we know is right and persist in doing what we know is wrong.
In the scriptures, this phenomenon is called killing the conscience.
The great scriptures of yoga—*The Bhagavad Gita, The Yoga Sutra,*
and *The Upanishads* clearly describe how the subtle causes of external war emanate from the internal world. The real causes of war lie
rooted in the individual's unwillingness to listen to the voice of the
heart, the inner conscience.

LOOKING INTO SUBTLE CAUSES

Soldiers are not alien beings; they are our relatives and neighbors. Their thoughts and feelings are like ours. Fighting is their job,
but if given a choice, they will avoid violence the same way a civil-
ian will. The duty of a soldier is to protect the other members of society from harm, and the government officials who order them to
fight are also doing their duty, which is to guide, govern, and preserve the social order. Violence does not originate with soldiers or

the governments that employ them. It originates with the most basic unit of society—the individual.

Every child is born into a religious structure; a well-defined group awareness; a certain economic class; a particular race, caste, color, faith, and creed; and a set of superstitions and dogmas. This creates a sense of divisiveness, and the moment a child enters the world, the parents begin to impose it on their offspring. Thus, we enter the world already entangled in a web of labels and identities, which we gradually come to believe and to mistake for ourselves. We grow into adulthood wedded to these superficial identities, a sense that "I am" one trait or another.

Our entire value system is shaped by the elements we have absorbed from our upbringing. Differences in values arise from differing backgrounds, and because we identify with the values that have been imposed on us, those with different values become a threat to our sense of "I-am-ness." Even the higher values of love and compassion are confined to those who share our values. That is why we preach love and compassion while judging and hating those who do not belong to our own little group.

We believe that we value universal brotherhood and sisterhood, but our concept of brotherhood and sisterhood is quite limited. If a wife and husband of two different faiths quarrel over which religious values to teach their children, and finally settle the matter by divorcing and splitting up the children, what can you expect of two different cultures? Have you ever heard of a Muslim adopting a Christian child and raising that child as a Christian? That would be a miracle, and the person raising such a child would be a great soul.

According to yoga, there is a collective awareness just as there is an individual awareness. A family is made of its members. A community consists of several families, a society of several communities, and a nation of several societies. Just as children in the family fight over toys, families and communities also quarrel with each other.

A community stands on a common ground of shared values.

3

On the basis of these values, it distinguishes itself from other communities. During the years the ego is developing, every child thinks that he or she is better than other children. The same tendency can be observed with communities. Ideally, as human beings and communities mature, they leave behind trivial matters. But this is possible only if the most important factor—ego—is transformed, expanded, refined, and polished. Ego, "I-am-ness," is the greatest barrier to the transformation and development of an individual at a personal level and, therefore, of society at the collective level.

This is where yoga steps in. According to yoga, the primary task of the individual is to overcome the trivial sense of "I-am-ness," or *asmita*. As long as we are stuck with the idea of "I am good," "I am bad," "I am Christian," "I am Muslim," "I am American," "I am Indian," "I am superior," "I am inferior," "I am poor," "I am rich," we can help neither ourselves nor others. Instead we remain embroiled in the exhausting chore of feeding the ego we have mistaken for ourselves, while holding the mask we have assumed firmly in place.

In order to satisfy the ego momentarily, we judge others and take delight in interfering with their lives under the illusion that we are uniquely qualified to set them straight. Because we are unhappy with ourselves, we attempt to force others to submit to us, hoping that their submission will convince us of our worth, and thereby increase our happiness.

Every community and society consists of those who are absorbed in this deception, and collectively such individuals create a grander, collective ego. There are many such collectives—ethnic groups, nations, sects, and factions of every persuasion. It is because of this collective ego that communities form nations and nations form alliances. It is because of this ego that East and West, First World and Third World emerge.

The Yoga Sutra, one of the most important yoga texts, says that attachment and aversion evolve directly from this sense of "I-am-ness." No matter how terrible our self-image, it is extremely difficult to shed that image and replace it with a healthier one because of the powerful attachment to that original sense of "I am." Because of this attachment, we are reluctant to examine this sense of "I am" to discover whether it is real or not. And because of this attachment, we delight in imposing the superficial grandeur of our "I-am-ness" on others. If others resist, we feel angry. When others attempt to impose their egos on us or on others, we consider them to be competitors. When we notice that another's self-image consists of healthier and more attractive elements than our own, we become envious. Thus anger, animosity, and jealousy are born.

If the global community consists mostly of those who have not worked with their egos, there will be no end to war in the outside world. War is the result of the intrinsic vanity of both the individual and the collective ego of mankind. Ego suffers from poverty, vanity, and a sense of emptiness, and it attempts to mask this sense of void by acquiring worldly objects, name, fame, dignity, and status. Lacking internal fulfillment, it tries to compensate with objects that do not belong to it in the first place. History is replete with examples of land, wealth, and property being used to compensate for inner emptiness and to satisfy the ego's vanity. Under the influence of vanity, the ego claims ownership of objects which were not earned through rightful means, and comes up against other egos making the same claims. Thus, the interests of two individual or collective egos clash, and peace and harmony are destroyed.

According to the yoga scriptures, ego has an enormous appetite. The name of that appetite is desire. A human being has insatiable desires, and in the process of fulfilling them, forgets that others are gripped by the same uncontrollable appetites. The ego forgets that it is impossible to possess the whole world. It forgets that others have the same urges and that therefore, its impulses will clash with those of others and lead to chaos.

How much land does a king, a shah, or an emperor need? How much wealth does it take to satisfy one who craves wealth? What is the highest status and the most potent symbol of power that a

5

power-hungry person can achieve? There is no limit. Unless we come to understand the self-defeating nature of our own possessiveness, we cannot stop making war.

It is useless to try to figure out who is right and who is wrong, who is good and who is bad. The pressing task is to create a state of well-being, a state of individual and social health, of peace and concord—a state in which all forces, all tendencies, all elements can come into harmony and human beings can live together peacefully.

Possessiveness is a sickness. The accumulation of excessive material objects is debilitating. This is true at both individual and collective levels. A society that is deprived of higher spiritual values substitutes a purely materialistic worldview, and as a result loses the ability to discriminate between real needs and uncontrolled desires. Such a society fails to share the gifts of nature and the gifts of God with the rest of humanity. History is laden with examples of this malaise.

This is not to say that yoga encourages poverty or discourages worldly prosperity. Yoga simply says, "Remember, this whole world with all its objects has evolved from God and still exists in God. Every single object, every single aspect of this world is pervaded by God. Things of the world are given to you as gifts. Learn to enjoy them without becoming attached to them. While enjoying the objects of the world, make sure that you do not covet others' wealth." (*Isha Upanishad*, verse 1)

Once we understand that everything has evolved from that single truth and that everything in this world is pervaded by that one truth, we will not fight over objects. The knowledge that we have these worldly resources at our disposal and yet we are not their owners will protect us from disputes and disagreements.

The problem is that our self-centered ego does not allow us to adopt a perspective from which such a conclusion can be derived. Thus, we are left with the problem of how to manage our selfishness, ego, greed, and desires. These subtle problems can be solved neither through political negotiations nor with sermons. They are the subtle causes of our external catastrophes, and the only way to overcome them lies in applying spiritual tools and committing ourselves to the disciplines that lead us to self-transformation.

A pragmatic politician may argue "Well, this is all very noble and philosophically soothing, but how does it apply to the emergencies of the moment?"

A yogi would respond: "General awareness is more powerful than the decisions of an individual or a handful of people. The enlightened multitude can stop the injustice brought about by a handful of people. Didn't Mahatma Gandhi lead a peaceful war in South Africa and India and finally win, not only the war, but also the hearts of those who staunchly opposed him? Such a thing can be done. It requires courage, tolerance, forbearance, endurance, and a total commitment to practice the philosophy one professes, but it is possible. The great scripture, *The Bhagavad Gita,* says, 'Peace is priceless. Attain peace at any cost.'"

The pragmatist will counter that this is all very well but it does not solve the immediate problem, and furthermore, it takes a long time to create a new, nonviolent collective awareness. In responding to such arguments, we must remember that what we are concerned with is not the current problem, but the future. Even if it takes twenty years, fifty years, or a hundred years to create the collective awareness of nonviolence, it will still be a noble achievement and we should set about it now.

THE CONSEQUENCES OF HATRED
AND REVENGE

We must shed the delusion that it is possible to attain peace through unpeaceful means. Think about it: both parties are convinced that they are fighting for a just end. Both parties are supported by people who believe in similar goals. When a war is fought, lives are lost and natural and man-made resources are destroyed. It is true that in the modern world many nations come for-

ward after a war with aid and funds for the damaged countries, but
no amount of aid will heal the emotional injuries or quell the hatred
in the hearts of the survivors.

The injury and oppression people suffered during World War II
still lingers, even after the lapse of almost half a century. Hatred for
the oppressors persists, engendering unrest and violence in countries
like Serbia, Kazakstan, and various Middle Eastern nations. After any
war, vengeance and hatred are like molten rock seething underground.

The post-war period, the so-called "peace period," is the time
when the magma of revenge and hatred begins to form. Sooner or
later, it is bound to explode into war. The magma breaks through
the weakest spot, turning that region into a volcano. There are
many such weak spots in our global society.

It is important to provide humanitarian aid when the volcano
explodes and to ease the misery of those who are in its path. And it
is vital to bring such an explosion to an end as skillfully as possible.
The crucial task, however, is to prevent the magma from accumu-
lating again, and this can be done only by eradicating the fear,
greed, selfishness, and anger from which the magma of revenge and
hatred arises. This requires an approach that has the power to effect
a qualitative and dramatic transformation—a "spiritual" approach.

This transformation must begin with the individual. Only this
will give rise to a transformed society. Whenever we ignore the
need for individual transformation and emphasize social transformation instead, a political or religious movement usually results,
and transformation gives way to social reform or a sect of some sort.
Eventually the leaders become ensnared by ego and vanity, and the
movement either collapses or its integrity is compromised.

8   A spiritual approach to individual purification and transformation runs no risk of sacrificing the higher values. It is more lasting
than social transformation. And once the number of individuals
who have transformed themselves reaches a critical mass, social
transformation takes place automatically. Furthermore, individual
transformation has an immediate effect on the lives of children,

whereas a mass movement affects only adults. What we do for our children is critical because it lays the groundwork for individual and collective transformation of future generations.

Individual transformation has the further advantage of being easier for our families, societies, and nations to absorb. The higher virtues can be developed gradually, and society can be spared the shock of revolution. Revolutions, even for the best causes, always create unrest and usually involve bloodshed. Individual transformation avoids such cataclysms. It is for this reason that Buddha repeatedly proclaimed, "Light your own lamp and the lives of others will be illuminated effortlessly." None of us has the power to force others to rid themselves of darkness. The only power we have is to demonstrate how delightful it is to live in the light.

According to yoga philosophy, there is a method for attaining inner peace and illumination, and there is a method for letting this light shine forth. It is a method that gently unfolds the virtues of nonviolence, love, and compassion.

Genuine transformation requires that we close the chasm between our worldly life and our spiritual life. Only then can we hold dual citizenship in two worlds—the world without and the world within. For this reason, the ancient masters invented a method of transformation that simultaneously affects every aspect of life: body, breath, mind, soul, and interpersonal relationships. It involves paying attention to what we eat and how we eat; paying attention to how we think, behave, and communicate with others, how we view this world, and how we maintain our status and position without threatening the status and position of others. This method is the practice of *ahimsa*—nonviolence.

9

PREPARATION FOR TRANSFORMATION:
EIGHT PRACTICAL STEPS

As with many other powerful yoga practices, nonviolence requires preparation. It requires the proper mental state, for it is im-

possible to practice nonviolence with a disturbed mind. Contemplation, which consists of eight steps, is the proven means for calming
and clearing the mind. If followed, it will engender a worldview and
philosophy of life that will support the practice of nonviolence.
Right thought, right resolve, right speech, right conduct, right
livelihood, right effort, right mindfulness, and right meditation are
the eight steps. What follows is a glimpse of the method of applying these principles and making them an integral part of your life.

Choose a specific time every day to practice these contemplative techniques. Make yourself available at that time, free yourself
from worldly concerns, and attend to the thoughts and feelings that
arise lovingly and respectfully. As you contemplate these principles,
try to feel what you are thinking. This is a dialogue between the un-
awakened and wakened soul within you. You are both orator and
audience, teacher and student, counselor and client. You are both
subject and object. As the thoughts flow and emotions are evoked,
let them form themselves as tears or smiles; let them manifest
silently or verbally; let them stir your entire being. Let the deepest
core of your heart be touched by these contemplative thoughts. Do
not reserve any privacy. Let the spirit of Buddha, Christ, Krishna or
Moses sink into you and expand your sense of "I-am-ness" beyond
the realm of boundaries.

In the beginning, you might simply read through the words
that follow. Later, it will not be the words, but the content of the
words that pervades your mind, uplifts your soul, and transforms
your entire being. At that stage, no one can tell you how much time
you should spend in contemplation. It becomes your wealth, and
where your wealth is, there your heart will be also.

one
right thought
Sit comfortably in a tranquil environment, preferably with your
head, neck, and trunk straight. Withdraw your mind from external

sounds. Focus on yourself—your body, your breath, and your mind. For a moment think of those who are near and dear to you. Recall the circumstances of the life you are living. Select a particular area of your life and reflect on how permanent or transitory it is, how much pain or pleasure it involves. Now begin the dialogue with your mind:

Mind, what makes you miserable? Worldly objects? Friends or foes? Losses or gains? Don't you realize that everything, including yourself, your beloved ones, and all the objects of the world are impermanent? In this short span of life, you get attached to things and to people; you create expectations that cannot be fulfilled by anyone. You forget that you have come to this plane to accomplish something, and after accomplishing it you will leave everything behind and move on. You mistake the impermanent for the permanent; that is why your expectations are so high. And, mind, if you don't change your attitude, you will end up with the same frustrations you have experienced many times in the past.

Objects of the world are neither painful nor pleasant. In their absolute sense, they are neither good nor bad. Conditioned to time and place, everything in the world, including our fellow beings, keeps changing its shape, behavior, and attitudes, and thus, from moment to moment, different characteristics of the same thing manifest differently. You expected that your car would always run smoothly—that was your mistake. So when it got a flat tire today, you got upset.

Mind, you must learn how to work hard and yet take it lightly. You must learn how to love others selflessly, without any expectation. You will find delight only when you do what you are supposed to do without expecting others to do what they are supposed to do. If they fail to do what they are supposed to do, that is normal. Drop your habit of blaming

11

and criticizing others. Listen to the sage who asked: "How many people are there in the world who magnify a virtue the size of a mustard seed in a fellow being into the size of the Himalayas and thus see only the virtue?"

Mind, it is entirely up to you what you look for and therefore, what you find. Change your attitude. Look for good; you will find it. Seek contentment; you will find it. Search for happiness; you will find it. This world is filled with everything you want—good or bad, pleasant or unpleasant, right or wrong, pain or pleasure, friends or enemies. What you search for is entirely up to you.

two
right resolve

To contemplate the means of making a right resolution, prepare your environment and compose yourself as you did for the first practice. Postpone worldly concerns and withdraw into yourself. This second step is meant to help you assimilate the theoretical knowledge that you have gained so far and to strengthen your determination to practice the higher values that you have abstracted from a spiritually grounded philosophy.

Recall an incident in which you did something which you knew at the time you should not have done, or taken a wrong action that you could have easily avoided. Recall the entire sequence of thoughts and events and contemplate:

How poor is my resolution, that in spite of knowing what is not right for me, and in spite of my decision not to do such things, I did this. Mind, it is due to the weakness of your resolution and determination. Mind, wake up, gather your strength. Remember and act.

This stage of contemplation is a means for acknowledging the stronger part of yourself and making the best use of it. Any sensible person knows what is right and what is wrong. At a conscious level, no one wants to get involved in an unhealthy and painful act. And yet, how easy it is to take such actions because of weak resolution and frail determination. By studying your own mind and heart and observing your strengths and weaknesses with the help of right resolution, you enable the stronger part of yourself to conquer the weaker part.

three

right speech

After establishing yourself in right views and right resolve, you must find the appropriate tools for expressing these views and this resolution. The first step is speech itself. Before our worldview and resolution can coalesce in action, it is reflected in our speech. Those who cannot discipline their speech will have a difficult time expressing their inner virtues through action. Speech is the coordination point between thought and action. It is the greatest vehicle of communication. Therefore, a person on the path of self-transformation should occasionally contemplate right speech:

How quickly words slip from my mouth. How easily my habits of speech permit me to forget my resolutions. How powerfully my words affect others. And how strongly others' words affect me.

During casual conversation, how much effort do I make to maintain my awareness of my philosophy of life and the higher values I have nurtured? How spontaneously and effortlessly my words express the contents of my mind. And in my effortless, spontaneous expression, what attitudes slip from my lips most often?

13

The predominant attitudes slipping from the mindfield through your speech reveal the contents of your mind. If the contents are not positive, creative, and healthy, then try to find some powerful antidotes—positive, creative, and healthy thoughts. These are also in the mind—it is simply a matter of unfolding them and raising them to the level of conscious awareness.

During this contemplation, recall instances in which you spoke in a manner that you regret. What were the emotional impulses behind this verbal outburst? This inner analysis of your habits of speech is a powerful means for studying your own thoughts and subtle behaviors, and thereby improving your relationships with yourself and others.

four
right conduct

Right resolve and right speech automatically lead to right action. But because our resolution is not always strong and because we do not always control our tongues, it is necessary to pay attention to our actions. Day and night, a human being acts. There are no exact formulas for performing these actions, but if we keep the following five virtues in mind, we can learn to perform our actions skillfully and properly. The five virtues are: nonviolence, truthfulness, non-stealing, non-sensuality, and nonpossessiveness.

It is important to spend a few minutes each day evaluating your actions and determining whether they have harmed anyone. What was the quality of your actions? How much lying, cunning, and cheating were involved? How tenaciously did you grasp your share? How many actions that appeared loving on the surface were motivated by your sensual desires? Which of your actions were driven by greed? When you find your actions and behaviors relatively free of these stains, reward your mind:

> Thank you, Lord, for dwelling in my heart in the
> form of conscience and inspiring me to do only that which
> is right.

When you find that some of your actions are causing pain to others, involving you in lying or taking what is not yours, or are

14

motivated by sense gratification or greed, sit down and have a dialogue with your mind. But do not condemn yourself; that will only weaken you. These are simple mistakes made by every human who has ever lived. They are not unforgivable sins. Sit quietly and have a dialogue with yourself:

Lord, give me strength and guide my mind and heart in the right direction. Let me be aware of the higher values of life which truly give me solace of heart. Let me acknowledge the tricks of my mind and my silly actions so that I may overcome them once and for all. Tell me, my Lord, why I forget the things I know and thus end up doing the things I don't want to do.

This stage of contemplation is important because it will lead you to discover if you are honest or hypocritical. The pitfall, however, is that it can create guilt, and we start condemning ourselves. Guilt and self-condemnation cripple inner strength and undermine self-confidence, so acknowledge your wrongdoings but do not judge. Find the flaws in your conduct and delight in your ability to discover these flaws, for according to yoga, self-discovery is its own reward. This stage of contemplation enables you to discover your true image, positive or negative, and gives you the strength to transform yourself.

Self-transformation is more effective than working with a priest or a therapist. Self-transformation enables you to become honest with yourself and when you are, you do not care whether others acknowledge your honesty or not. Attain firm grounding in the principle of right conduct, and you will automatically understand the importance of right livelihood, the next step of the practice.

15

five
right livelihood
This contemplation requires you to understand the basic law of life: whatever is born needs food and shelter. All creatures—pigs and

shrews, tigers and moles, elephants and squid—find nourishment and refuge. But somehow humans no longer have a natural way of obtaining these things. Although they have learned to survive in any climate, so far they have not found a way of earning their livelihood while maintaining peace and harmony among themselves.

According to the scriptures, all domestic quarrels originate in the kitchen, centering around food and drink, gradually spreading into other areas of family life. Unrest in a nation or among nations is also rooted in the quest for food, shelter, and other types of sustenance. The roots of cheating, stealing, and deception can be traced to how one makes one's living.

Many human beings fail to confine the idea of "making a living" to obtaining food and shelter. Just as individuals are engrossed in "making a living," so are businesses, communities, and societies. And in order to acquire more, they will capture land, plunder the wealth of their neighbors, and even enslave others.

We each must contemplate the purity of our livelihoods. The best measure of "right livelihood" is the peace and harmony you maintain while earning and enjoying your living. The less disturbance you create in your own heart and in the lives of others, the more "right" your livelihood.

The following contemplation is a means of assimilating this principle and living with this truth:

Is my livelihood compatible with my worldview and my philosophy of life? Am I really happy with the work I do and the money I earn doing it? If not, is it just a mental habit of mine to be unhappy with whatever I do, or is it the quality and effect of the work itself that makes me unhappy? Am I questioning my work because I don't get along with my co-workers or because I feel that I am underpaid? Or am I uneasy with the quality of the work itself?

Am I harming other beings in the course of earning my livelihood? Am I damaging the planet or creating pain or hostility in others? If so, is there any alternative? Am

I sharing the fruits of my endeavor with those who are karmically connected with me? How balanced is my life in regard to what I accumulate? Am I really enjoying the fruits of my labor or am I overindulging myself? To what extent do I remain aware that all the objects of the world are simply meant to make my life comfortable and peaceful so that a greater amount of time and energy can be directed toward attaining the highest goal of life? Is my livelihood serving this purpose or has it become a goal in itself?

six

right effort

Those who are trying to live a balanced and harmonious life through right views, right resolve, right speech, right conduct, and right livelihood still face the deeply rooted subtle impressions of their past deeds that are stored in the unconscious mind. These play a significant role in daily life. They motivate our conscious mind, senses, and body, and as a result, there are times when we fail to do what we know is right. So powerful psychological and spiritual tools—yogic methods of meditation, contemplation, and prayer, and a number of breathing exercises—have been developed through the ages to conquer and transform these subtle tendencies hidden in the unconscious mind. All of them require effort. Nothing can be accomplished without work.

Each individual must decide which technique or combination of techniques will be most helpful—meditation, contemplation, prayer, study of the scriptures, the company of more evolved souls, or self-analysis. Applying the following process of contemplation will enable you to discern which will best help you deal with the subtle tendencies in your unconscious mind. Sit quietly, close your eyes, and ask yourself:

When I am not successful in the process of self-discovery and self-improvement, is it because I lack a clear

17

understanding of my right view, right resolve, right speech, right conduct, and right livelihood? Or am I clear about these issues but lose my balance and create a mess for myself because of my strong sense cravings? Or do my old habits and unknown subtle tendencies of my unconscious mind keep me from doing what I know is right? Am I too much influenced by my environment and the company I keep, and am therefore unable to organize myself and lead a healthy life? What is it that is stopping me from creating the kind of life I value?

If this process leads to the realization that your problems stem from confusion about right views, resolve, speech, conduct, and livelihood, then studying the texts, further contemplation, and the company of those who have a clearer knowledge of these things will all be helpful. If you notice that your problems are due to your uncontrolled sense cravings, then you need a systematic method of dealing with your body and mind. A discipline consisting of a balanced diet, exercise, deep yogic breathing, a schedule for going to bed and getting up, and gradual withdrawal from the objects of sense gratification will be helpful. If you are creating trouble for yourself with your habits, you need a systematic method of meditation. If your environment and companions are the source of your problems, the remedy lies in seeking the right environment and in living with people who are spiritually aware.

seven

right mindfulness

You must keep your mind occupied with thoughts that are healthy for you and helpful to others. The mind is an energy field that cannot be emptied—it must contain thought constructs. If you do not deliberately supply it with healthy thoughts, then it pulls content directly from the bed of its memory without discrimination. And if your storehouse of memories does not contain pleasant and spiritually elevating thoughts, you will end up thinking destructive thoughts that will wreak havoc in your life. An empty mind is the devil's playground. Before the devils have a chance to play their wild games, build a temple for the Divine so that it can shine forth instead. Practicing the following contemplation, once or twice a day, even for a few minutes, will help purify the mind and fill it with joyful thoughts.

What are the thoughts that constantly and involuntarily occupy my mind and heart? Why do such thoughts come into my mind? How trivial they are, and yet I cling to them, thinking they are clinging to me. Mind, drop this delusion.

Another approach is to ask yourself:

Why, in spite of constantly cleaning my mind, does it still become filled with trash? It must be because I'm doing only half the job. I empty the mind, but because I do not fill it up again with positive thoughts, the trash comes up to fill the vacuum. Therefore, let me occupy my mind with constructive thoughts, remembering that the great masters of the past have said that constructive thoughts are twofold: constant awareness of the evanescent and trivial nature of worldly objects, and the knowledge that the purpose of life is Self-realization—not hand-to-mouth, office-to-bed existence. Therefore, mind, never forget that you are on an eternal journey. Don't get lost in the scenes you see. Keep the destination in mind.

Mind, in the procession of life, do not waste your time fighting with others and holding others back so you can get ahead. Walk on the path humbly, gently, and skillfully, with full focus only on the goal. Have compassion for those fellow travelers who surround you. Let them walk with you. If you have a better understanding of the map and the goal, humbly share your knowledge. If possible, give them a ride.

19

And remember, at all costs, don't be confused by thoughts of distinction between "mine and not mine." Mind, allow me to always remember that I am on an eternal journey.

Thus, let the mind be filled with the awareness of the Supreme Goal. This is right mindfulness.

eight
right meditation

Right meditation deepens the contemplative truths that are practiced at the level of right mindfulness. Because the mind is accustomed to perceiving things with the senses, it is difficult for the mind to comprehend Truth, which is subtle, dissimilar to worldly objects, and does not come through the senses. It is necessary, therefore, to present a comprehensible idea of the Truth for the mind to grasp. And for this reason, Truth is given different names and forms in different spiritual traditions.

It is best not to superimpose many commonplace characteristics on the concept of truth, for such superimpositions are the basis of cultural and religious differences and thus are the source of strife. And because none of the symbols for Truth or God that have been invented by the human mind perfectly describes the nature of Truth, the yogic tradition prefers to avoid symbols or images. Yoga simply refers to Truth as "Pure Consciousness." Pure existence, pure consciousness, and pure bliss are intrinsic to Truth. Or, as Buddhism expresses it, Truth is characterized by wisdom and compassion.

It is of utmost importance to use a system that carries the fewest possible cultural and religious biases when you meditate on Truth. For example, light can be used as a symbol of Truth; meditating on light twice a day is a powerful means of keeping the mind focused on Truth. Meditating on the principles of love and compassion is also helpful, for wisdom unfolds in the kingdom of love and compassion.

THE PATH OF MEDITATION

The path of meditation can be systematically subdivided into three parts—concentration, meditation, and perfect spiritual absorption. The first step is to concentrate on the idea or principle itself—in this case, light or the principles of love or compassion. But before it is possible to resolve to concentrate on a principle, one must have an intense interest in it, and this comes from understanding its value. Because of this zeal, the aspiring meditator attends to the idea itself, or to a teacher or to a book explaining it. The degree of attention determines how concentrated the mind is on that principle, which in turn determines how firmly it is grasped. A firm grasp and a burning desire to live with the principle enables the aspirant to retain it in his or her mind for a prolonged period.

Prolonged retention is the essence of meditation. The difference between concentration and meditation is the length of time the object of concentration is retained in the mind. For example, if the mind retains the object for the time required to complete twelve inhalations and exhalations without another thought intervening, that is meditation. And when the mind is so absorbed for this twelve-breath period that it is not aware of anything at all, that is called perfect spiritual absorption *(samadhi)*.

a method of meditation

Sit with your head, neck, and trunk straight. Place your hands comfortably either on your knees or in your lap. Withdraw your mind and senses from the external world. Mentally observe your body and the place occupied by your body. Then, once your body is still and your breath is steady, visualize a flame either in the area of your heart or at the point between your eyebrows. At the first glimpse of light in either of these two regions, offer your love and respect to that light as the representative of the highest truth within and without. Pay your homage: "Great Eternal Light, enlighten my path and the paths of

21

all. May we all walk on the path of Truth without stumbling. Shine so brightly that we may see Thee even from this shore of life."

After paying this homage, let your mind focus on the light. The moment you notice that your mind is wandering, and therefore that your focus on the light has become unsteady, immediately re-solve to bring your awareness back to the light.

Your concentration will be enhanced if you pay attention to your breath. While inhaling, imagine that you hear the sound "so," and without creating a pause, begin exhaling and hear the sound "hum." "So" simply means "that"; "hum" means "I am." Keep breathing and listening to the sound "so hum" with full awareness of its meaning, "I am that, I am that.'" As your awareness deepens, the meaning also expands and you may feel:

I am that Light, the Divine Light, I am that Light that shines in all individual hearts. I am that Light which is the purest and the most accurate image of the Supreme Lord, the Almighty.

I am that Light. My true essence is that Light, not the physical appearance that I carry all the time. There may be differences in our external appearances, but deep down, we are one and the same. All living beings are pure Light. That Light alone is life. Let me honor that life. Let that Light enlighten my life and the lives of all. Peace, Peace, Peace.

THE FRUIT OF PRACTICE

This eightfold path of contemplation, which culminates in meditation on Truth, makes the mind one-pointed and purifies the heart, filling it with love and compassion. Nonviolence flows spon-taneously from such a heart.

And once we, as individuals, are established in the principle of nonviolence, our society will no longer be ruled so completely by fear and greed. We will no longer need police forces or armies. Free from all enemies, we will finally attain freedom from the most implacable enemy of all—war itself.

This ideal state of nonviolence represents the highest stage of human evolution. Although we have not yet evolved to such a sublime state of consciousness, there is power in visualizing ourselves at this pinnacle. If we long for peace, we must aspire to it. To attain it, we must set to work with great energy. That is the only way we will ever free ourselves from both the war within and the war without.

I object to violence because even when it appears to do good,

the good is only temporary; the evil it does is permanent.

—Mahatma Gandhi

NONVIOLENCE:
THE ANTIDOTE TO WAR

MANIFESTATIONS OF VIOLENCE

In the yogic tradition, the word for "nonviolence" is *ahimsa*, which means, literally "not hurting, non-killing, not damaging." But none of these phrases accurately captures the profundity of the concept of ahimsa. Ahimsa (which I will translate as "nonviolence" in the interest of brevity), connotes non-harmfulness at every level of existence. There are philosophical, ideological, and spiritual injuries, as well as physical, verbal, and psychological ones. Ahimsa connotes nonviolence at all these levels simultaneously.

The most obvious form of violence is physical violence. It is the outer manifestation of the subtle violence that we carry within and usually fail to acknowledge.

In some ways, physical violence is easier to contend with than verbal violence, and can actually be less damaging. Physical abuse is palpable, and its effects are immediately visible. Therefore, it is likely to be brief. Those who commit this form of violence immediately notice what they are doing and often realize their mistake, and this realization is usually enough to snap them back to a quasi-normal state. If not, then someone else often intervenes.

Verbal violence is less tangible, so it will probably continue longer. Physical violence harms the body, but verbal violence affects a deeper level of being—the mind, the emotions, and the spirit. In a verbal fight the effects are long lasting. The wounds inflicted in a physical fight can be treated with antiseptics and bandages, but the wounds inflicted by speech are not so visible and cannot be so easily treated. If the verbal injury is not treated immediately, an infection begins that sooner or later will erupt in more violence.

Verbal violence is rooted in mental violence—before we hurt others with our speech, there must be a violent thought in the mind. These violent thoughts are not the result of intellectual analysis; they stem from an emotional outburst, which momentarily overrides the faculty of discrimination. As long as our reactions are discerned and restrained by the faculty of discrimination, we behave peaceably; but if our emotional reactions are not screened by the discriminative faculty, we behave wildly. And in most situations, we react on the basis of our emotional impulses.

This problem is exacerbated when our emotions are controlled, not by wisdom but by another emotion—fear of being punished, for example, or the desire to stay on good terms with someone in power. Repressed emotions are the ground for mental violence, and in this fertile soil both verbal and physical violence germinate.

Violence at a psychological level originates in the form of a negative thought, such as hatred, anger, jealousy, or the desire for revenge. If this negative thought does not find expression, those who hold it become volatile. Negative thoughts are painful, and without a healthy means for expressing them, the thinkers remain in pain. Because they have little self-knowledge, they will not understand why they are unhappy and will seek an outside cause. As a result, at the merest excuse, they will accuse someone else of causing their troubles. If the other person denies the accusation, a verbal battle ensues. Unresolved, it can escalate and become physical.

Violence can also take philosophical or ideological forms. Those who are convinced that their ideas are the only valid ones may not only attempt to impose them everywhere, but may also vehemently condemn the ideas of others. This is often seen in disputes between two scholars, philosophers, or teachers. A religious crusade is an example of ideological violence, as are disputes over political and economic systems.

Spiritual violence is also common. Taking the Truth for granted, spiritual teachers sometimes misguide their followers. In a sense, this is spiritual violence, but in this sensitive area, being specific could cause great offense. And this would in itself be a form of violence. That is why, in the realm of spirituality, silence is often considered to be the best policy.

THE ANIMAL, THE HUMAN, AND THE DIVINE

All forms of violence are common among human beings. But this is not ordained—violence among humans is not inevitable. Far from being an intrinsic part of our nature, as is commonly assumed, violence is an aberration.

According to the scriptures, every human being is born with three qualities—animal, human, and divine. During infancy and early childhood all three tendencies manifest, and seek an environment in which to grow and find expression. And because there is a divine being, a human being, and an animal within each individual, a baby can be raised as a sage, as a gentle loving human, or as a criminal. Through proper training, education, and loving guidance, however, the beast within can be transformed first into a pet and then into a human. The same human can later expand his or her consciousness and become divine.

If the parents have not freed themselves from the negative forces of attachment, anger, hatred, jealousy, greed, and fear, and thus do not care for higher virtues, such as selflessness, love, compassion, and generosity, then the animal tendencies will be strengthened in the child they rear. If the parents nourish these animal tendencies, the child will grow outwardly as a human, but inwardly as an animal, and will exhibit animal behavior as an adult.

The scriptures say that humans and animals have four qualities in common—the four primitive urges of hunger, sleep, sex, and fear (the desire for self-preservation). All emotions spring from these four primitive urges. The degree of control one has over them marks a being as either human or animal. Fear and hunger seem to be the most dominant of the four primitive urges because animals devote most of their energy avoiding their predators and searching for food.

All four urges play a key role in the lives of humans, but in most cases, much of our behavior is controlled neither by these urges nor by the emotions they generate. The faculty of discrimination balances their effect on our actions, and to some extent, we have the capacity to subordinate our individual urges to the needs of others. But if we allow these urges to drive our behavior they will consume us, and we will become self-serving, defensive, and fearful. These are animal tendencies. Rising above such tendencies—by cultivating concern for others and deepening our sensitivity to the needs of others, even in the face of self-serving urges—elevates us from animal to human. And from here, we can unfold the higher virtues of selfless love and compassion, and move toward the Divine. But we can become divine only after we have become fully human.

THE GENESIS OF FEAR

According to yoga, the process of training and taming the animal within, transforming it into a human, and then into the Divine is accomplished by the practice of nonviolence. Its transformative power can be understood by examining the relationship between violence and fear, and between nonviolence and fearlessness.

Fear of death is the greatest of all fears. All others are pale shadows of this primal terror. Fear of death is innate to anything that is born—humans, animals, insects, and even plants. Every living being has developed defense mechanisms in response to this inborn fear, but other species focus more of their energy on developing their defense mechanisms than do humans. This, according to yoga, is because they are consumed by fear. In humans, there are many other tendencies to balance the survival instinct.

Seeking to understand fear, the yogis searched for a cause and found twins—attachment and aversion. A human being forms a more powerful bond with family members and pleasing objects than do other animals. But this strong attachment to some people and things automatically results in aversion to other people and things. Humans constantly strive to achieve what they like and to rid themselves of what they dislike, and it is usually a personal sense of liking and disliking, rather than need, that makes us characterize an object as good or bad. Humans are afraid of not getting what they want and of ending up with things they do not want. And because humans are highly developed beings, their wants, desires, likes, and dislikes are legion. There are more sources for their fears than for other, less-evolved species. One sign of evolution is the development of a self-identity—the sense of "I-am-ness." A human being is a conglomerate of numberless identities, and each individual's sense of I-am-ness includes myriad elements such as good, bad, healthy, strong, rich, poor, Hindu, Moslem, American, European, wife, husband, son, daughter, and so on. Within each of these identities, an individual carries an enormous burden of likes and dislikes, attachments, and aversions. Each element of this burden creates a fear that some part of the identity will be lost or taken away, or that an unwanted identity will be imposed on it.

All fear can be traced to attachment and aversion, and attachment and aversion can be traced to self-identity, the sense of I-am-ness, or ego. Our inclination to defend or attack has its genesis in our fear of losing something that we believe to be integral to our

29

identity. Just as pain is a symptom of disease, violence is a symptom of fear. Fever counters threats from a virus or bacteria, and violence counters threats to identity. Fever and violence are both indications of an internal struggle. An uncontrolled fever can jeopardize life, as can violence. And as long as there is fear and the cause for fear, violence will recur. The more fearless we are, the more nonviolent we become.

The freer people are from fear, the more open they are. Those who are fearful are sealed in their own little world, and as a result, they suffer from a sense of emptiness and loneliness. But those who are free from fear are open and loving. They have minimized their attachments and aversions, and so they are naturally less caught in the idea of losing and gaining. Thus they are free of stress and tension, and remain tranquil in all situations.

THE CYCLE OF VIOLENCE

When nonviolent instincts are overridden by negative, violent forces, humans become even more dangerous than creatures in the wild. Fortunately, such an occurrence is rare—only a fraction of humanity cripples its human virtues by nourishing the violent tendencies of the animal within. Violence is an aberration, and all societies have methods of isolating overtly violent individuals.

Humans are usually nonviolent. Even hurting or killing our enemies is something we normally avoid. Usually, others make these decisions on our behalf. The question is, who are these others? Are they really so different from us? Are they not our representatives? And as our representatives, they must represent what we feel in some way. At some level, we are all involved in violence. At some level, we seek it and delight in it; otherwise, war and bloodshed would not be so widespread.

Violence cannot be abolished by assigning the blame to someone else. We can stop it only by examining our own thoughts and feelings. Human beings are masters of self-deception. To avoid listening to the voice of our own hearts, to lighten the burden of guilt, and to justify our inhumane deeds, we use distancing language to describe our actions. For example, we use the word "casualty" to refer to maimed or slaughtered humans and "collateral damage" to refer to the maiming or slaughtering of civilians. Such language allows us to remain comfortable with the consequences of war and to obscure the facts so the public doesn't become sickened by the violence and demand an end to it. But denying our destructive tendencies or hiding them with sweet-sounding words will not change them. As long as the root of violence remains, it will find expression.

We must stop pretending that it is possible to end war and violence with war and violence. Short of a nuclear holocaust, there can be no "war to end all wars." The past has shown us that the seeds of the wars to come are planted in the current war. The mind has a penchant for remembering the event but forgetting the lesson, so we must train our minds to remember the lessons and somehow forget the events. The memory of the events evokes the irrational causes behind them, and thus the perpetrators of irrational acts are never forgiven. And because in any war each side considers the other to be the irrational perpetrator, the stage is set for the next act of destruction.

THE POWER OF NONVIOLENCE

Nonviolence is the only constructive strategy for engaging the enemy. Before, during, and after its application, it remains nondestructive and non-painful. Nonviolence is the only weapon that renders B-52 bombers, Scud missiles, and "Smart" weapons impotent. Practitioners of nonviolence are the only soldiers who attain ultimate victory. Nonviolence is the only force that transforms an enemy into a friend: the winner surrenders to the loser, the loser to the winner, and both attain victory.

The practice of nonviolence begins with individuals, and because "similar attracts similar," it spreads, pervading the community,

31

then the nation, and finally the entire human race. It is a slow process but a sure one. It is long-lasting and has no adverse side effects.

People often argue that we need a leader like Buddha, Christ, or Gandhi to initiate a war of nonviolence. A yogi would respond that there is a Buddha, a Christ, and a Gandhi in each individual heart. A part of every individual is as enlightened, merciful, compassionate, loving, and fearless as Buddha, Christ, or Gandhi. Such souls incarnate at the call of the compassionate and nonviolent forces within us.

Each time we call, a Buddha emerges among us. The Bible says, "Ask, and it will be given." But the Bible doesn't specify what to ask for and therefore what will be given. A collective consciousness asked for Saddam Hussein and got him. A collective consciousness called for George Bush, and he's there.

We get whatever we ask for. God Almighty is immeasurably generous, but He must shudder when we silly children ask for knives and cut our fingers. God has nothing to do with what we do to ourselves. We can use the gifts, the grace, and the intelligence that have been granted us for either right or wrong. We often use it for wrong—sharpening our intellect and using it to exploit nature and each other for selfish ends.

This is where we violate the principle of nonviolence. Possessiveness and nonviolence are incompatible; nonviolence walks hand-in-hand with selflessness. Hatred and violence, love and nonviolence, giving and receiving, accepting others and being accepted by others—these are perfect pairs. Knowing this and living in the light of this knowledge is the key to nonviolence.

A proponent of nonviolence knows that a peace that is only the gap between two wars is a superficial peace, and that deep beneath the peaceful surface, hatred, anger, greed, ego, possessiveness, and the desire for revenge brew and seethe. During the gap between two wars, nations and factions race to build or acquire arms—a race that is simply preparation for the next war.

During wartime, when the volcano is erupting, it is almost impossible to practice and teach nonviolence. In the midst of war, people are obsessed with winning the war or escaping its consequences. It is during the period of peace that the real work of fostering nonviolence can be done. During a war, providing food, medical care, and money will save lives and ameliorate the immediate suffering, but cultivating nonviolence during the interval of peace will spare future generations the horrors of war.

The power of nonviolence is beyond the grasp of an ordinary mind. Darkness cannot face the brilliance of nonviolence. If the human race is ever to coalesce into a harmonious society of peaceful nations, it will do so on the firm ground of nonviolence and selfless love. But mere belief in the principles of nonviolence is not sufficient, because even now, most people in the world believe in nonviolence. But wars still rage because nonviolence is an abstract principle to most of us, a passive belief rather than an active part of our lives. Making it active requires living it in thought, speech, and action.

Just as soldiers are trained in precise methods of finding and striking military targets, so are there precise methods of practicing nonviolence and targeting the injured areas of our lives at both the individual and the collective level. These techniques bear no resemblance to the practices in psychiatric institutions where violent people are rendered inert with drugs and other methods. There is nothing inert about nonviolence. It is a demanding way of life that is supported by a sound philosophy and fueled by spiritual practice.

CULTIVATING NONVIOLENCE:
NINE CONTEMPLATIVE PRACTICES

If practiced sincerely, the following contemplations will create a firm grounding in the principles of nonviolence. They will enable us to transform ourselves and gain a better understanding of ourselves, our friends, and our "enemies." They will also help us to cultivate a positive worldview and sound philosophy of life. In the initial stages of this practice, participants will benefit individually; its influence will gradually spread.

The sages of the past have promised that when you become peaceful and happy, love and compassion will radiate from you. People will bask in your light and warmth and wonder why you are so pleasant and loving. This curiosity will lead them to observe your lifestyle and ask about your philosophy. They will want to know your secret, and because the secret is so simple—don't hurt yourself and don't hurt others—they will begin to emulate you. And that is how the power of nonviolence emerges from the heart of individuals and begins to pervade the family, the community, and society as a whole. One day it will surely pervade the whole human race. But first, individuals—you and me—must begin practicing the principle of nonviolence systematically. This is not a religious commandment; we must not impose this principle on others. This is not a business strategy; there is no need to penetrate the market. This principle is a nectar, and wherever there is nectar, honeybees gather because nectar sends a silent invitation to all honeybees. Let us begin to gather it.

one
nurture your conscience

We kill our conscience when we continue to do things we do not want to do while postponing the things we want to do. Working against the conscience creates an internal battle—the inner self is split, each part warring with the other. And once this inner conflict is underway, your mind becomes utterly confused. It wavers back and forth between right and wrong, just and unjust, without establishing a firm ground anywhere.

Those with confused minds are vulnerable to emotional appeals and can be swayed by sensational speeches. They are entranced by demagogues and tend to join mass movements without giving much consideration to whether or not the cause is good or just. If the cause is unjust and they come to realize it, they feel

34

guilty. And guilt leads to self-condemnation, which in turn perpetuates the process of killing the conscience.

The practice of nonviolence begins with cultivating the conscience, and once the seed has been sown, truth will sprout. The first step is to take time to listen to the voice of your heart. Periodically, once a week if possible, put aside all opinions about disturbances in the external world—international crises; political controversies; or conflicts at work, in the community, or with your family. If your nation is at war, try to find time for this practice every day. For five minutes, drop all thoughts of enemy, friend, nationality, race, or gender from your mind. Find yourself on common ground with your opponent—both of you are humans. And holding that perspective, try to discern what your relations are with your opponent and how balanced your reactions are. Listen to the voice of your heart, the voice of the soul, which has equal love and concern for both of you. Your heart will tell you what is right.

When you hear the voice of your heart, don't allow your mind to become frightened. Mind is accustomed to being selfish, egotistical, and skeptical. Just as one army disrupts the radio transmissions of another by jamming them with extraneous noise, so the mind transmits static to garble the voice of the heart. Do not allow your mind to create interference. The fewer noises created by your mind, the clearer the voice of your heart. And the clearer the voice of your heart, the closer you are to Truth. The fewer fears you have of losing your selfish objectives, the longer you will retain the light of Truth. A burning desire for Truth and reverence for life itself will help you create the environment in which you can contemplate these matters.

35

two

cultivate tolerance

Differences in geography, terrain, vegetation, climate, and natural resources have engendered different ways of life. Studies by anthropologists and philologists show that to a great extent each culture's religion, philosophy, customs, superstitions, and other values are shaped by these factors. And viewed from this perspective, every way of life has its own reason for being and its own integrity. We make a mistake when we use our own cultural standards to judge the values of another culture. For example, we consider cultures with fewer material objects—automobiles, televisions, telephones, and indoor plumbing—to be "poor." Similarly, we think those who are unfamiliar with our convoluted economic system and our complex technological society are ignorant. In both cases, such people may be richer and wiser than we are, in terms of contentment, honesty, truthfulness, peace, and happiness.

One of the main causes of violence is the tendency to label others and pass judgements on their way of life, especially when this is done with the intention of imposing our ideas, value systems, and lifestyles on them. Even if it is done with the best of intentions, an adverse reaction is inevitable. Every community identifies itself with a set of social, cultural, and religious values, and develops an attachment for them that often borders on reverence. Challenging these values is tantamount to challenging the identity, the sense of "I-am-ness" of every member of the community. Those so challenged will respond with fear and anger.

The failure to understand that others' values are as important to them as ours are to us breeds intolerance. Tolerance is the cushion that absorbs the shock of our mutual differences, and once that cushion is gone, the impact can be brutal. In the absence of tolerance, the impulses that lead to violence thrive.

Tolerance is integral to nonviolence. The following contemplation is one way of assimilating this principle:

> Look at the diversity in the world. Certainly it is part of nature. If diversity were not natural, then God would have designed all the mountains in the same fashion. All humans would have the same faces. People everywhere would have the same skin tone. But how boring and redundant that would be. It is the same with lifestyle and

values—it is natural for humans to express their diversity in that way too.

Let me not condemn how others think and what they think. It doesn't matter whether or not their values are profound and meaningful to me. Let me learn to respect them and their beliefs exactly the way I want others to respect me and mine.

three
be nonjudgmental

This is an expansion of the principle of tolerance. The concepts of virtue and vice, merits and demerits that we nourish in our minds, cloud our vision. We forget that most values are conventional, subject to time and place. That which seems virtuous today might not seem virtuous tomorrow. Similarly, we make such statements as, "These Americans always . . . ," "Arabs never . . . ," "Buddhists usually . . . ," or "South Africans don't . . . ." That is how we create prejudices in our mind and why we jump to conclusions about others on the basis of partial or erroneous information. Sweeping generalizations are absurd at best and dehumanizing at worst: not all people in the Himalayas are sages; not all Americans are decadent; not all Muslims are seeking martyrdom; and not all prison guards are brutal.

Many prejudices are subtle, but they manifest in our thoughts, speech, and actions. Often we fail to notice them at all, or if we do, we may not consider them to be significant. But when the time comes to interact with other groups or to make decisions regarding them, these subtle traces of our prejudices surface and prevent us from seeing these "others" in their full complexity and humanness. 37

Violence has its roots in prejudice and the habit of creating labels. And when one group dehumanizes another by applying pernicious labels, war is imminent. Often this is done deliberately to make the "enemy" seem as alien as possible so that killing them will be less appalling.

The following contemplation is one means of eradicating the tendency to label and dehumanize others:

How can I judge the children of God whom he created in his own image? Let me not label any of God's images and discriminate against them because to do so shows disrespect for the Creator. Let me examine the purity of my own heart instead. Let me observe how skillfully I refrain from cultivating prejudices against those who do not belong to my religion, faith, creed, and culture. Let me remember that we are all children of God and that each person is an individual, just as I am. And let me refrain from harming anyone through my thoughts, words, or action, no matter how different from me they seem.

four

remember the lessons events teach

The human race is divided into many groups, each with a sense of its own history. Just as calamities make newspaper headlines, the events most likely to be recorded in the history books are the dramatic, emotion-provoking episodes. And history, like every other area of life, is subject to interpretation and manipulation. So far, there is no complete or accurate history of any group or series of events, and we end up studying partial histories and projecting the selective version of recorded events into the present and the future.

As a result of remembering and studying their various histories, Hindus, Jews, Muslims, and Christians have nourished ill-will toward each other. We recall and recount events of the past and try to punish the descendants of those we believe oppressed our ancestors. This is folly. We must learn to forget the events while remembering the lessons those events teach. Let the historians pursue their research; let them dispute one another's findings and argue about who did what to whom and whether or not it was justified. But for our own good, the rest of us should close the sad and vengeful chapters of the past to prevent them from poisoning the present. This is the only way to free ourselves from the anguish and vengeance passed down from generation to generation.

Instead of pondering over the injustices of the past, whether real or imagined, let us contemplate:

We all are members of the same species. We live on the same planet, consume the same food and water, breathe the same air, and walk in the light of the same sun. We fight over the same things because we all are human and share the same hunger, thirst, and fear. How sad it is that we remember only the wars and other disputes and forget the good things we share and the feelings we have in common.

It is a tendency of the human mind to keep careful track of negative, destructive, violent activities and spare barely a moment's thought for the good things. We must reverse this tendency and learn to retain only the good memories and let the trash be swept away.

Let me find a way to do this, no matter what others do. Let me transform myself, and let me change my habit of remembering specifics about my family, clan, and race, especially in relation to people I have formed a habit of disliking as well as those who I believe dislike me.

five

cultivate love, compassion,
and nonviolence

Within the confines of a single community whose people share common religious, cultural, and economic values, it is necessary to honor those values. But it is important both to recognize that many of our own values are conditioned by time and place, and to honor the values of other communities—even when they are radically different from our own.

39

The values of universal love, compassion, and nonviolence are perennial and supersede all others. If conventional values conflict with these universal values, the universal values take precedence. Conventional values are the means of maintaining law, order, and harmony within communities, but the higher values of love, compassion, and nonviolence are the means of bringing the smaller communities into a bigger fold. The higher values are the means of expanding our consciousness and teaching ourselves to focus on the interests of all humanity rather than centering our attention on the narrow interests of the group with which we identify. Here is how to contemplate this point:

I am a human—that is my primary identity. How can I subordinate my human identity and the human identity of others to the secondary identities of gender, ethnicity, nationality, religion, and political philosophy?

Do not let my likes and dislikes, my attachments and aversions toward these secondary identities obscure the virtues of love, compassion, and nonviolence. Let me remember that, no matter how it may appear, the similarities between me and every other human in the world far outstrip the superficial differences.

six
remember all entities are interdependent

All beings, including all humans, are interconnected at one level or another. It may seem that we live independent lives, but this independence is supported by a larger interdependence. This is apparent in the international community. One nation's economy influences the economy of many other nations.

The global communications network has made all members of the human race much more familiar with each other than we ever were in the past. It is no longer possible to hide either our richness or our poverty, our love or our hatred, our good or our bad intentions toward each other. It is becoming clear that all humans are part of a single global organism, and it is crucial that we learn to act and communicate in perfect peace and harmony. Unrest in any enclave immediately spreads across the globe.

If we grind our teeth in our sleep and wake up with a headache, we don't destroy our teeth in order to teach them a lesson. Instead, we recognize that this behavior is a symptom of internal stress and set out to find the cause and the cure. So it should be in the outer world. Just as we grind our teeth in our sleep for a reason, there is a reason why a segment of humanity causes pain to the rest. Any outward expression of violence is a symptom of internal stress. But instead of condemning the members of a group for being violent and either punishing or destroying them, it is better to find and uproot the cause of the violence.

One way of removing the source of stress is to find a better way of understanding and communicating with each other. Just as all organs of the body must function together in perfect coordination to ensure the health and well-being of the organism, all segments of the human community must work together to promote the well-being of humanity—if the mouth keeps food for itself, if the heart collects and hoards blood, if the lungs capture and stockpile air, the body is doomed.

The same is true of the organism of humanity. The major international problems—poverty, pollution, and political unrest—come into being because one part of the organism treats another like an alien being. We forget that others are an integral part of ourselves as we unwittingly enfeeble ourselves by weakening others and depriving them of their share. The following contemplation is a means of assimilating this knowledge:

How am I connected with others, and how am I separate? Can I really exist apart from those who seem to be physically separate from me? Can humanity exist apart from humans and/or humans from humanity? Not at all.

There is a forest and there are trees in the forest. Are the trees completely different from the forest? It doesn't

41

seem so. All the trees and shrubs—small and big, green and dry, those that bear fruit and those that are barren—make up the forest. If each tree and shrub is separated and removed, the forest no longer exists.

It is the same with humans and humanity. And yet, how profound is our ignorance when we believe we can damage the trees without harming the forest. Let me love all and live with the knowledge that everyone is part of me and that I am part of everyone.

seven

remember there is only one life force

Although we may be able to live separately at the physical level, one life-force runs through us all. It sustains every aspect of existence—the world of minerals as well as the kingdom of plants, animals, and humans. All sentient beings need food, air, water, light, and heat, but these elements have no preferences about who they nourish. They simply serve as vehicles of life energy, and in doing so, they create a greater bond among us than we commonly realize.

The air we inhale travels through every cell of our bodies, gathers not only toxins, but also thoughts and feelings, returns to the lungs, and is exhaled through our nostrils. All that we know at the deepest level of our being passes into the air outside our bodies. That air is then inhaled and assimilated into the systems of others, where the same process begins again. Those who have developed their higher sensibilities experience the thoughts and feelings of others simply by coming into contact with the air in the atmosphere around them. Such is the nature of our existence and the depth of our mutual sharing.

By either polluting or purifying our minds and hearts, we affect others. By affecting others, we ultimately affect ourselves. We can blind ourselves to this truth, but we cannot change it. According to the sages, whatever we do to others will be done to us—we reap what we sow. Hurting others is hurting ourselves; loving others is loving ourselves. There is no difference between us; the same life-force animates us all. A person who wants the love, respect, and honor of others must love, respect, and honor others.

It is obvious that a single force endows all beings with life. This single life-force sustains us all in its dazzling diversity. I know this, and yet somehow I fail to see myself as an integral part of creation.

Why do I act as though I'm blind to the unity that underlies every aspect of existence? Let me love all in the full knowledge that loving all means loving myself, because under the surface there is no difference between me and all other beings.

eight

know that hurting anyone
means hurting God

According to each of the world's great spiritual traditions, all individuals are children of God. From early childhood we have heard the phrases, "All men are brothers," "Love thy neighbor as thyself," and "We are all God's children." Yet still we condemn and injure others. Just as parents are saddened when their children fight and injure each other, so must God be saddened when we hurt one another. Remembering that hurting any of God's children is tantamount to hurting God will help us remember to treat one another with kindness and love. The following contemplation is helpful:

Mind, cast off your selfishness; it allows you to injure others. If you claim to love God, then you must not disappoint Him by hurting those whom He loves. You must not dishonor Him by dishonoring those whom He adores. He loves and adores not only me, but every woman, man, and child on the face of the earth. By showing love to all His children, I show my love for God.

43

nine
honor divine law

Law and order are necessary if humans are to live together in groups. Rules governing behavior vary from culture to culture and even among groups within one culture. So when making rules and setting standards for behavior, we must be careful to define the boundaries of our group and to respect the boundaries of other groups. In the scriptures, the ground for performing one's duties is called *karma ksetra*. Just as there are individuals, societies, communities, and nations, so are there individual, communal, societal, and national "fields of duty," and people may experience internal conflict when one field of duty overlaps and contradicts another. For example, the mother of a baby may find her individual field of duty in conflict with her societal and national fields of duty if she is also a soldier and her country is at war.

External conflicts arise when, in the performance of duty, the field of action of one individual or group intersects with that of another. Most of our troubles arise when we believe that the performance of our duty requires us to interfere with others who are also performing their duties.

When this happens at the group level, war is often the result. Although justifications can usually be found, it is extremely difficult to know whether or not this interference is really necessary. This problem cannot be solved by the intellect alone. Intuitive wisdom, grounded in love, compassion, mutual understanding, and nonviolence is the best means of knowing whether or not we should intervene in the lives of other individuals, communities, societies, or nations. But because our intuitive wisdom is often buried under our selfishness, ego, fear, and attachment to our own conventional values, we often intervene when we should not and create turmoil for ourselves and others.

It is even difficult to contemplate this point, because without repeated practice in overcoming ego, selfishness, attachment, and aversion it is impossible to even see the problem. But we can pray to a higher power or to the Divinity within to give us the strength and wisdom to overcome our blindness so that we can walk in the light of divine law.

God, give me the wisdom to see that others have duties just as I have. Let me learn to be wary of my tendency to believe it is my duty to interfere with others. Before acting, let me always stop and examine whether the impulse to intervene springs from ego, fear, or attachment to my own values, or from compassion and selfless love. Lead me to the sublime state of consciousness where I know, through my own direct experience, that my true family is the human race. Let me embrace all and exclude none.

May I learn to delight in sacrificing my personal pleasures for the sake of my family. May I learn to sacrifice my family interests for the welfare of the community, and may I find the wisdom to sacrifice my communal interests for the welfare of my society. May I envision the ways of contributing to the welfare of the entire humanity, even if I have to sacrifice the welfare of "my" society.

Defend yourself against your enemies,

but do not attack them first: God hates the aggressor.

—The Koran (2:190)

WHEN WAR IS INEVITABLE

There are times when war seems inevitable and there are times when fighting seems to be a duty—much depends on the angle of perception. Even if war is inevitable or just or both, killing one's enemies runs counter to a basic tenet voiced by all of the world's great spiritual traditions. Consider Christ's urging to "Love your enemies"; the commandment "Thou shalt not kill" that God passed to the Jews through Moses, and the yogic advice to practice *ahimsa.*

Justifications have always accompanied war. Through the centuries they have coalesced into a set of principles that have found their way into international law. According to these principles, in order for a war to be just it must be declared as a last resort by a "legitimate authority," and then only to support a just cause. Wars of aggression are never justified, although international law recognizes the legitimacy of wars waged to counter grave threats to international order or those joined on behalf of a helpless third party.

None of these justifications bears close scrutiny. What some call a "legitimate authority," others will call an outlaw government. What one nation views as a just cause, another nation will view as an outrage. And the "last resort" may never be reached because it is always possible to convene another round of talks. All of these points are controversial and subject to intellectual and emotional argument. For every person espousing one view, there is someone eager to refute it.

Like other philosophical and spiritual systems, yoga has grappled with the question of when war is justified. The sages recognized that when the forces of violence and destruction seize power, war may offer the only solution. But even then it is almost impossible to sort through the options objectively and be certain that taking up arms is the correct choice.

The mind is tricky and loath to know itself. Even the most conscientious thinker is prone to unconsciously twist ideas and facts to suit a preconceived notion or to justify a course of action. Making the correct decision about whether or not war is justified requires profound analysis and scrupulous self-study. Those with whom the decision rests must exercise discrimination, listen to the voice of conscience, and analyze the facts honestly.

According to yoga, even if this painstaking process leads to a decision to declare war, the opponent must still be given many opportunities to back down. The scriptures say that if war is imminent because of domestic issues, and if both parties are part of the same family, then the participants must forgive their opponents one hundred times before using force.

These scriptures were written long ago when monarchs ruled and kingdoms were inherited. Wars were fought over possession of the throne and often involved brothers. But even though the particulars are different today, the essence is unchanged—the drive for power and possessions and the agony and chaos that attend war are the same in any century. *The Bhagavad Gita,* one of the great yoga scriptures, tackled the question of when war is justified in the third century B.C. According to legend, the profound wisdom of the *Gita* was imparted between the front lines of two opposing armies just moments before a great battle was to begin. The following translation and analysis of a portion of this text explains when and why fighting a war becomes one's duty and gives us a sense of the complexity of this problem.

THE ROAD TO WAR

There once was a king who yearned to renounce the world and devote his life to spiritual pursuits. So, entrusting his kingdom to his brother who was blind, he retired to the forest with his wife and young children. Soon after he arrived, however, he died and the queen returned to the court with their five sons. These children and the children of the blind regent were raised and educated together as brothers. But when the oldest son of the rightful king reached manhood and was ready to assume the throne, his blind uncle was reluctant to step down. So the rightful heir, who was generous and peace-loving, agreed to let him keep the throne for the remainder of his life. But that only fed the uncle's greed.

The blind regent hatched plots to ensure his own son's succession and his sons made several attempts on the lives of the rightful heir and his four brothers. Scheme followed scheme, and things went from bad to worse. But throughout it all, the rightful ruler refused to resort to violence. Finally the wicked uncle and cousins contrived to exile the five brothers to the forest for thirteen years.

During this period, the false king and his sons gathered an enormous military force, stockpiled weapons, and formed alliances with neighboring countries. Their subjects were miserable—taxes were heavy and every penny was used to increase the strength of the army; corruption was rampant; and women and children were not protected. People prayed for the rightful king and his four brothers to return from exile, so they did. The rightful king sent an emissary to the court with a proposal for getting his kingdom back; the emissary was mistreated and the proposal spurned.

49

Finally, Krishna, a man of the highest wisdom and a great king in his own right, undertook to settle the dispute. He went to the court of the wicked king with another peaceful proposal, but it too was scorned. Undaunted, the five brothers made yet another attempt, sending Krishna to say that they would be content with one village apiece, but the king and his eldest son refused to yield even a pinpoint of land without a fight. And so it went for several years— Krishna and the five brothers trying to find a peaceful way to restore order while the wicked king and his sons thwarted every attempt.

Eventually all diplomacy was exhausted. Nothing was left but to go to war. And so the day came when the two opposing armies were massed on the battlefield, eager to fight. But even then, the rightful king wanted to be sure that fighting this war was right and necessary. So he asked his younger brother, Arjuna, the best among all warriors, to ride out to take a final look at those who were arrayed for battle.

THE DIALOGUE
BETWEEN KRISHNA AND ARJUNA

The great soul, Krishna himself, was the charioteer. At Arjuna's urging, he drove to the center of the battlefield, and what Arjuna saw was devastating. There with the opposing army stood his own grandfather, his teachers, cousins, nephews, and numberless other relatives and friends ready to kill and be killed. His mind was flooded with grief. How could such a battle be anything but evil? In his despondency, Arjuna turned to Krishna, and the following dialogue took place:

"Oh Krishna," Arjuna cried. "The best of the youth of both kingdoms stand here on this battlefield. Intoxicated by the opium of war, they have lost their senses. They think of nothing except killing. They are excited; they are blinded; they would rather die than retreat. And many of them will die—we will lose the better part of an entire generation of men.

"And that is only the beginning. When the war is over the true

50

catastrophe begins. Many in the older generation will die from grief; the younger generation will be bereft of guardians. Mothers, wives, and sisters will be without protection. People will suffer from the scarcity of food and clothing. Disease will thrive, and there will be no one to treat the sick. Children will inherit only sadness and grief. Revenge and hatred will stalk the land.

"Don't you see, Krishna? This war will create a gap of three generations among us. It will shatter the civilization, culture, and knowledge which has flowed in an unbroken current from generation to generation for thousands of years. With the passage of time, the intensity of grief will subside and the normal human urges will return. But an entire generation of women will have no partners.

"Krishna, you must stop this war. I prefer to retire to the forest and live as a monk rather than fight and gain a victory at such an unbearable cost—the loss of life, culture, civilization, natural resources, and ultimately, the wisdom of our ancestors."

"What possesses you, Arjuna?" Krishna replied. "Now is not the time to think of these things. The boundaries of these noble thoughts have already been crossed, and that is why we now stand on this battlefield. Even if you retire to the forest, these armies will clash. If, overwhelmed by these noble and peaceful thoughts, you do not fight, you will bear the entire responsibility for the destruction that will be wrought by your enemies. Even those that you lead are no longer in the mood for peace. These armies will spill each other's blood, no matter what you do. At least let righteousness triumph amidst this destruction.

"If you lead this army into battle, Arjuna, you might not get credit for the victory, but if you refuse to fight, you will certainly be blamed for failing to defend peace and justice. It's a bad bargain, but what can you do? That's the nature of life."

"You take life so lightly, Krishna!" Arjuna replied. "Can you really justify destruction and violence? Aren't we fighting for a piece of land and wealth? How can you value either of these more than life and peace?"

"Arjuna, you are walking backward." Krishna answered. "These are the thoughts that should come before armies gather, not in the midst of a battlefield. These questions are not flowing from the center of wisdom; they are only the manifestation of your attachment to your kinsmen, teachers, and friends.

"If your blood were not royal, it would not be your duty to lead a battle for kingdom and property. But your blood is royal, and you must preserve justice and order for the sake of your people. If you fail to do your duty, multitudes will suffer. Arjuna, in this light you are not a person, but a champion of essential human needs. You defend others by defending yourself. You must fight to protect others. This war is a means of avoiding a more severe and long-lasting injury. You must get up and fight."

"But Krishna," Arjuna objected, "is nonviolence conditioned by time and place and circumstance? Is its application so limited? Tell me, oh my wise friend, when should one practice nonviolence and refuse to fight, even in self-defense? When should one defend oneself with arms? When should one surrender to the situation, and when should one try to change it by any means possible—either peaceful or unpeaceful?"

Krishna said, "This is a profound question, Arjuna. There are two main ways of meeting any situation. All other ways come in between. These are the way of the tortoise and the way of the ocean. I will explain each of them to you.

"Just as a tortoise, sensing a threat, withdraws into its shell and so remains safe, Arjuna, a human being should withdraw to safety when threatened. A tortoise never complains. Neither does it attack. Even if it receives a pounding, it does not fight. Yet it always wins because sooner or later the enemy retreats in frustration. But with humans, the victory is even more complete, because a human enemy will be affected by the virtue of tolerance, forbearance, forgiveness, and passive resistance, and may even become a friend.

"The difference between a human and a tortoise is that a tortoise is helpless and cannot choose to fight its enemy, whereas a human is not helpless and yet refrains from fighting. There is more power in voluntary inaction arising from the principle of non-violence than in involuntary inaction arising from helplessness.

"So listen carefully, Arjuna. The way of the ocean is a higher path than the way of the tortoise. The ocean never rejects the waters of any river, whether polluted or clean. It allows all rivers to merge into it and, embracing them all, absorbs them as integral to itself. Such is the action of a human of the highest wisdom and greatest strength, one who includes all and excludes none, loves all and hates none. People from all walks of life, people with different philosophies, abilities, and virtues are all embraced by the oceanic personality of such a one.

"Such people do not withdraw into protective shells when encountering a threat from enemies; rather, they open the door of love and compassion and make themselves available to be loved or tortured. Even if they are being crucified, they utter no word of complaint. These are the people who transform society. Their inner strength surpasses the strength of millions. They are the torchbearers of the human race.

"You see, Arjuna, there are different paths for different people. The way of the ocean may better suit a renunciate or monk than the way of the tortoise. But the way of the tortoise is more suitable for one who has yet to transcend the confines of family, caste, and community, one who has yet to unfold the full breadth of inner strength and understanding. Each person must examine his or her own knowledge, understanding inner strength, tolerance, forbearance, forgiveness, and compassion, to discover how best to apply the principle of nonviolence. Ultimately, Arjuna, the only competent guide is one's own conscience, as long as it is not contradicted by common sense and the higher welfare of others."

"But Krishna," Arjuna replied. "It doesn't answer the question of when to surrender to the situation and when to try and change it."

Krishna replied, "It is simple, Arjuna. Surrender to the situation if your personal life alone is affected. But take action if the lives

53

of others are involved. If such a situation demands the use of force, use force."

"Yes, Krishna, but how do you justify the violence that attends the use of force?" Arjuna asked.

"Because you are a great man and you hold no animosity toward anyone," Krishna told him, "you must adhere to the way of the ocean. This is your personal path for private spiritual unfoldment. But you are more than a private person; you are also a public person entrusted with the welfare of the multitude. Personally, you have no enemies because you are not contaminated by feelings of animosity. But the enemy of society, the enemy of the multitude, is absolutely your enemy. For the sake of humanity, this enemy must be vanquished.

"For your personal spiritual unfoldment, follow the path of the ocean, which is the path of the sages. But for the sake of humanity, follow the path of the noble warrior. By creating a balance between these two paths, you incur no sin in killing. Such action is called 'the action of an inactive person.'

"Fighting in a war while deep down practicing the principle of nonviolence, is like rowing two boats at once. But only a master can row two boats and still reach the other shore safely. Such a task demands perfect balance between emotional reaction and rational decision. And you are the only one who can judge if you are successfully rowing two boats or if you are a hypocrite."

But Arjuna was not convinced. "Still, Krishna," he said, "this war, led by me and supported by a man of supreme wisdom like you, sets a dreadful example for future generations. My internal states—my thoughts, emotions, and beliefs—cannot be so easily transmitted to others. How can they discern them? People know me only through the example of my deeds. Some will take this example, and without understanding the subtleties of my internal states, they will use it to justify committing violent deeds for their own convenience."

"Arjuna, humans have the intelligence to know that which they wish to know," Krishna continued. "If they wish to blind themselves, they can contradict the principles taught by their elders, misinterpret the clearest precepts, or twist the wisest teachings out of context. People have done this before now, and they will do it again. These subtle principles are for those who have the courage to be honest with themselves and are willing to listen and understand.

"Therefore, Arjuna, do not take it amiss that your example will sometimes be exploited by the ignorant for their own selfish ends. No doubt you will be subject to harsh judgements, but that must not stop you from doing your duty. Defending righteousness and restoring law and order is your present duty.

"Don't degrade yourself to the point of impotence with these endless arguments, Arjuna. It's not like you. Rise above this momentary weakness of your mind and heart. Get up like a warrior. Defend those who look to you for protection."

THE WAY OUT

This dialogue makes clear how complicated it is to decide when to take up arms and defend righteousness at the cost of carnage and destruction. From one perspective, *The Bhagavad Gita* sets out to solve the riddle of war, but instead ends up wrapping it in an enigma.

The text presents the social, ethical, philosophical, and metaphysical reasons for fighting this particular war. These are thorny issues, and wise man that he is, Krishna skirts direct answers, discoursing instead on spiritual matters. Several times during the dialogue, Arjuna reminds his mentor of the practical issues at hand and asks for an unequivocal explanation of how it can be right for him to participate in a massacre that will destroy his kin, his race, and his country. But Krishna always reverts to metaphysical arguments—military council becomes spiritual instruction. This is because Krishna knows that spiritual knowledge is the only way through this morass and he continually directs the dialogue to the plane above the material.

Krishna urges Arjuna to fight, but will not do so himself. Although he insists that this war is necessary, he does not take up arms. He vows to stand with the forces of righteousness, yet he will not fight for them. He offers his presence, not his participation. The message implicit in this incongruity is that although human affairs may become so convoluted that war is inevitable, fighting will never eradicate the causes of war.

There are times when matters become so tangled that war is unavoidable even though it will not bring any permanent resolution. When a society is crumbling, laws are inhumane, people are suffering, and the only way to correct the situation is to overthrow the laws and the lawmakers; fighting may then become a duty. That is a matter for each individual to decide. But even so, winning the war is only part of the mission. After the victory it is crucial to find a way to restore harmony and justice. And this brings us back to the question of why human affairs become so convoluted in the first place.

The war in the *Gita* was instigated by possessiveness, as are most wars. And as long as possessiveness exists, it will lead to war. Excessive materialism is a dark corner in the human heart where the light of spirituality has not yet penetrated. In this realm of darkness we blindly steal what belongs to our neighbors, occupy each other's land, claim the fruits of others' labor, and attempt to satisfy our egos by dominating others and imposing our values on them. And until this darkness is banished, we will continue to wound ourselves and brutalize others.

To cleanse and heal ourselves, we must apply only universal principles of spirituality—those with the fewest religious overtones. Only practices involving the purification of mind and heart and acceptance of others as our own brothers and sisters are helpful. In Buddhist and yogic literature, contemplating these principles is called *Brahma vihara*—living in God consciousness. The next chapter offers a practical approach to doing this.

The wolf shall dwell with the lamb; and the leopard shall

lie down with the kid; the calf and the lion and the sheep

shall abide together, and a little child shall lead them.

—Isaiah 11:6

AFTER THE WAR: VANQUISHING HATRED AND REVENGE

Once the fighting is over, people breathe a sigh of relief, clear the rubble, and pray that they will never have to face the pain and sorrow of war again. This is a sad and futile prayer. There has been no victory; the enemy has not been defeated. The real enemy, war itself, has simply gone underground with its weapons—anger, hatred, jealousy, greed, and revenge—intact. But these deadly weapons are camouflaged by peace talks, political negotiations, territorial settlements, and war reparations. And because the spirit of war retains its weapons, diplomatic maneuvers are ultimately ineffective. War always resurfaces.

Somewhere deep inside, we all know this, but we refuse to act on our knowledge. So far no one has devised a strategy for truly disarming the enemy and transforming the subtle agents of destruction into the generative forces of love, compassion, and mutual understanding. Instead, we concentrate on repairing the physical damage and begin building better weapons to defend ourselves in the future.

After any war, everyone, both victor and vanquished, experiment with ways to channel their energies in peaceful directions. But unfortunately, these experiments are rarely constructive or lasting because we are attempting to create a new life with the same old mental patterns. And we again mistake sensual pleasure for happiness, material wealth for security, and chemically altered states for peace and relaxation.

Eventually we end up satiated with sensory pleasures, smothered in material goods, stupefied by alcohol and other drugs, and thoroughly dissatisfied. And not knowing what we are searching for and thus having no idea where to look, our energy flows into the same old grooves—dominating others, and trying to make ourselves feel powerful by forcing them to acknowledge our superiority. And so the cycle continues.

Once we recognize that the enemy is war itself, however, and make a firm resolution to defeat it once and for all, an enormous reservoir of energy becomes available. For example, the money and other resources that even a short war consumes can feed millions. The money required to build a B-52 bomber could also build a water treatment plant. The money spent in manufacturing gas masks could be used to educate children in one of the poorer nations. The time, energy, and ingenuity lavished on designing and testing a powerful new weapon could be used to develop an efficient irrigation system for a region stricken by drought. But do we really do such things? No—because we have not yet transformed our attitude toward ourselves and others. We have not yet really decided to live in peace and let others live in peace.

Like war, peace begins at the individual level. We will stop fighting with other communities and nations when we stop fighting with our families and our neighbors because the animosity created when home is a battleground infects the community and engenders a collective atmosphere of animosity, which in turn infects the community of nations and makes the world a battleground.

Those who are caught in personal and domestic battles either turn their anger inward and abuse themselves, or turn their anger outward, abusing their family members and quarreling with their neighbors. In either case, an atmosphere of hostility is generated which spreads in concentric circles. Jealousy, hatred, anger, possessiveness, and feelings of inferiority held at the individual level have the same effect as a stone dropped into a pond. The unrest ripples outward, disturbing the family, the community, the society, the nation, and finally, the community of nations.

It is not possible to quell unrest in the larger world until we have quieted our own restlessness. According to *The Yoga Sutra*, there are four principles, which if cultivated and assimilated, will free our minds from the disturbances created by jealousy, hatred, anger, possessiveness, and feelings of inferiority. These four principles are: cultivating friendship for those who are happy, compassion for those who are suffering, cheerfulness toward the virtuous, and indifference toward the non-virtuous.

In the beginning, it may be difficult to discern the link between practicing these four principles and dissolving the feelings of anger, hatred, and revenge that fuel violence in the external world. But with time and practice, the link will become clear, and our minds will become free of animosity and become established in God consciousness.

LIVING IN GOD CONSCIOUSNESS:
FOUR PRACTICES

To live in God consciousness is to live without fear, anger, hatred, jealousy, and greed. Cultivating friendship for those who are happy, compassion for those who are suffering, cheerfulness toward the virtuous, and indifference toward the non-virtuous has the power to give us this freedom. According to *The Yoga Sutra*, these principles can be practiced and assimilated through contemplation or through meditation. Either method will purify our minds and hearts. And this purification will be accelerated if we have the courage to face our fears, the determination to transform our lives, the company of like-minded people, and the grace of God.

one

friendship for those who are happy

Everyone wants to be happy. And if, while trying to attain happiness, we constantly find ourselves surrounded by others striving for the same goal, we regard some of our fellow seekers as friends and others as competitors. Toward still others, we remain indifferent. But for the most part, our own insecurity and other weaknesses lead us to believe that the fewer candidates for happiness, the greater our own chances for achieving it. Therefore, at some subtle level, we want to get rid of everyone, even friends, although life without friends is misery in itself. So, caught in the dilemma born of our own ignorance, we suffer from the pain we have created for ourselves.

There are endless permutations of this cycle. For example, when others succeed, even those we love, our own insecurity and feelings of inadequacy engender jealousy, and in subtle ways, our envy motivates us to attempt to destroy their happiness. Misguided by the tricks of our own minds, we sometimes delight in disturbing the happiness of others, even at the cost of making ourselves unhappy.

This convoluted behavior is not confined to a particular group. It is a widespread psychological disorder that cannot be cured by professionals. The only cure is self-transformation. What is required is an antidote for competitiveness and jealousy. And that antidote is the attitude of friendliness for those who are happy and successful. Contemplation is one means of cultivating this attitude:

60

> At least there is someone in the world who is happy. Let me learn to rejoice in the happiness of others. Let me walk on the path of happiness without elbowing others. Let me envision my happiness without clouding the happiness of others.
>
> Let me appreciate those who are already happy and

find ways to inspire those who are not. Let my happiness remain unaffected by others. Let me remember that the kingdom of happiness is infinite and eternal. If the whole world becomes happy, my happiness will grow rather than diminish.

Examine your own circumstances and see how you are creating misery for yourself by envying the happiness of others. If you have neighbors who appear more fortunate than you, cultivate a friendly attitude toward them in your own mind as well as in your outward behavior. In this way, you will begin to overcome your own feelings of inferiority, which are what torture you most.

Remember, this world is full of diverse beings, objects, thoughts, and feelings. Diversity is a law of nature, and this diversity is characterized by an unequal distribution of intelligence, strength, wealth, and the inexplicable phenomenon of fate or providence. Therefore, expecting everyone to be equally happy is absurd, for this is not the design of nature. But neither is it the design of nature for humans to shoulder the task of accelerating the inequality among themselves and disturbing the natural peace and harmony of the world with jealousy and strife.

A second, more powerful means of developing an antidote for competitiveness and jealousy is to meditate on the concept of friendship. By meditating on the virtue of amity, the sages tell us, one becomes the friend of all and the friend to all. Friendliness and animosity cannot coexist. The mere presence of one who is fully established in the virtue of friendship neutralizes animosity in the hearts of others. And in the presence of such a highly evolved person, one's internally held animosity washes away. This is called "the effect of company." The following story illustrates this point:

During the time of the Lord Buddha there lived a notorious cutthroat, the leader of a band of outlaws who roamed the land, terrorizing everyone in their path. The leader, the most ruthless of the lot, had sworn a solemn

61

vow to behead 1,000 people with his own hands and make a garland of their fingers. At last, having severed 999 heads from the shoulders of the innocent, he was impatiently seeking the ultimate victim.

One day, while ranging through the thick forest, his men fell upon a lone traveler. Although he offered no resistance, the brigands brought him before their leader at sword point, making no secret of the grisly fate that awaited him.

Eager to fulfill his vow, the chief drew his sword and growled, "First your fingers, then your head."

Unperturbed, the captive, who happened to be the Lord Buddha, extended his hands saying, "If you have need of my fingers, my friend, take them and use them as you wish."

The cutthroat, staggered by this man who, moments from agony and death, remained gentle and undisturbed, began to quiver with terror. Buddha continued to gaze at him with love. The sword slipped from the cutthroat's hand, and overwhelmed with remorse over all the blood he had spilled, he collapsed at the feet of the Enlightened One. Buddha touched his head, lifted him up, and in one loving embrace, he banished every impulse to cruelty the man contained.

The next morning the reformed cutthroat and all his men were ordained as monks. In Buddhist literature this monk is known as Ananda, the most beloved of Buddha's disciples.

Amity is an aspect of nonviolence. The clearest embodiment of this principle in modern times was Mahatma Gandhi, who taught his followers to "eliminate the animosity, not the enemy." Gandhi knew that the first step toward this was to perfect the principle of amity within himself.

While out for a stroll one day, he happened on a group of children at play. At the sight of this thin, half-naked, strange-looking man, the children took fright and fled. Gandhi, who loved children, called to them, hoping to allay their fears, but to no avail. So this great soul paused for a moment, searched his mind and heart, and concluded that a wisp of fear and animosity still lingered there, which caused the children to flee. So he set himself to fasting and purifying his heart until the magnetism of his virtue of friendliness grew so powerful that it pulled children toward him.

When it is perfected, the virtue of amity is so powerful that all fear and animosity evaporate in its presence. But its real gift lies in the power it holds to banish all traces of jealousy and competitiveness from the thoughts, words, and actions of all who are earnestly striving to instill amity in their own hearts and minds.

two

compassion for those who are suffering

Just as we pollute our minds and hearts with competitiveness and jealousy toward our happier and more successful neighbors, we also soil ourselves with feelings of superiority over those who are suffering. That same ego which is deflated by an encounter with someone who is happier than we are, swells at the sight of someone who is more miserable. And just as cultivating friendship for those who are happy dissolves competitiveness and jealousy, so does cultivating compassion toward those who are in pain dissolve vanity and feelings of superiority.

Feelings of superiority are actually feelings of inferiority cloaked in vanity. As feelings of inferiority increase, so does vanity, and sooner or later, this pernicious pair is bound to express itself in speech and action. Lack of concern for those who are less fortunate, scorning the unfortunate or feeling uncomfortable in their presence, and a general attitude of arrogance are the visible symptoms of feelings of inferiority.

As a result of these feelings, we build a thick wall between ourselves and those who are less fortunate. And because we fail to realize how damaging this wall is both to ourselves and to others, we continually add to it. Thus, balance is disturbed, differences increase, and the community fragments. The discontent that begins to smolder among those who are excluded inevitably blazes into hatred.

Honor and dignity are human birthrights, but blinded by ego, the happier and more fortunate among us fail to acknowledge this in those who are weak and suffering, suppressing them with our arrogance or indifference. Failing to acknowledge another's pain is an act of violence because people suffer when their pain is ignored; those who are ignored or suppressed feel compelled to assert themselves in the name of honor and dignity. And on the collective level, war is often the result.

When the sages studied this problem they saw that compassion for those who are suffering is the only remedy. But compassion is both subtle and profound. Most people confuse compassion with sympathy, but the resemblance between them is superficial. Sympathy is an emotional response to those in pain, and an emotional response presupposes identification. Compassion, on the other hand, is never accompanied by emotion and is an expression of pure, selfless love.

The internal state of the sympathizer is affected but a sympathetic response; the compassionate person remains undisturbed. The sympathizer is reminded (either consciously or unconsciously) of similar experiences in his or her own life; past memories are its major cause. The person who is suffering is simply the stimulus for the sympathy.

64 Compassion, on the other hand, is the fruit of wisdom. It is completely unconditional; selfless service and pure love are the springs from which compassion flows. One who is fully established in the principle of compassion expresses it effortlessly and is deeply concerned but unaffected. The compassionate person acts and moves on, with no interest in acknowledgement or reward.

In the process of learning to move from sympathy to compassion, the practitioner must be wary of acting on impulse and take care not to become caught in the act of compassion itself, as the following story illustrates:

A young monk, a disciple of the Lord Buddha, was sitting on the bank of a flooded river. As he watched the water swirl by, he noticed a scorpion drowning. Thinking to save its life, he impulsively plucked it out of the water with his fingers, and the scorpion promptly stung him. In surprise and pain, the monk dropped the scorpion back into the river, where it resumed drowning. Seeing this, the monk thought, "What else other than stinging can this poor fellow do? That's the way of scorpions."

Then, remembering the compassionate words of the Buddha, the inspired monk picked up the scorpion again, was stung again, and again dropped the scorpion into the river. This sequence was repeated over and over until every drop of the scorpion's venom had been injected into the monk. Only then was the determined young man able to hold onto it long enough to drop it on the river bank. Half dead from the poison and the pain, the exhausted monk collapsed beside the spent scorpion.

As they lay there, an old monk happened along, and the instant he saw the pair, he knew what had happened. He made a poultice for the youngster's swollen hand, and revived him. But as soon as he came to consciousness, the newcomer began slapping and scolding him. "Fool! Fool! Why invite such misery for yourself?"

The young monk was confused. "The scorpion was drowning," he said. "Haven't you heard our Lord's saying 'Compassion and love are the only wealth mankind possesses'? Selfless service is the law of life."

"Yes," the old monk replied, "It is true that you must perform your actions lovingly, compassionately, and self-

lessly, but most important, do it skillfully. This means, get
a stick and use it to fish the scorpion out of the river. Once
it's out, get away from it before it stings you."

We must learn to express our compassion through skillful
service, selflessly rendered. Then we must walk away. Lingering
compromises the virtue of selflessness, which is the essence of compassion. Suffering people have egos too and they need to retain
their sense of dignity. On one hand, they need help, but they do not
want to feel obligated or demeaned. Expect nothing, not even un-
spoken gratitude, from those to whom you render service. The ability to give is itself an act of grace, as the following story illustrates:

There once was a saintly Moslem poet named Rahim.
He was both very wealthy and very generous. Every morning he sat outside his door with an ample pile of grain,
clothing, and money for anyone who might have need of
these things. He offered these gifts with outstretched
hands and downcast eyes. He never saw the people who
received his bounty.

After this had been going on for years, another poet
asked Rahim, "Why are you so shy and timid while giving
these gifts? You seem almost to be ashamed."

Rahim replied, "All the objects in the world belong to
God. It is God who gives those objects to the needy ones
outside of my house every morning. He uses me as an instrument. I'm honored to be God's instrument. That's why
I feel shy. But people mistake me for the true giver. That's
why I feel ashamed."

Compassionate service helps to alleviate the pain of those who
are suffering. But its greater value lies in purifying the minds and
hearts of those who render it. The satisfaction and joy you derive

from rendering selfless service to someone in need is immense and everlasting. But there is one danger, and that is feeding your ego by identifying yourself as a generous, compassionate person. This is destructive both to you and to those to whom you render service. Compassion is authentic only if your kind words and deeds are accompanied by subtle feelings of selflessness, lack of ego, and transcendence of the sense that "I am the doer."

All these factors can be held in the mind in one integral thought contained in the following contemplation:

All these people—those who are poor and suffering— are also children of God. By serving them, I am serving God. Let them express their gratitude only if it gives them pleasure. But let me remember that I don't deserve a syllable of thanks for my kind words or good deeds—these are simply my duty. I am thankful to those I serve because it is through them that I have been given the opportunity to serve God.

Meditation on the principle of compassion is a means of erasing our own hatred, cruelty, and fear, and replacing these traits with love, kindness, and a deeper understanding for others. Those who meditate on compassion rise above the primitive urge of self-preservation, and thus their reactions toward others are not motivated by fear. Such people spontaneously and effortlessly understand and forgive others.

Those who are fully established in the principle of compassion know that the motivating factor behind most immoral, unethical, or non-virtuous actions is a lack of the basic necessities of life—in either the material, emotional, or spiritual realms. Therefore, no matter how many times a materially or spiritually impoverished person insults or harms those who are established in compassion, they continue to radiate selfless love.

three

cheerfulness toward the virtuous

Just as we want to be happy, we also want to be virtuous—or at least to think of ourselves as virtuous. Because of attachment, desire, ego, and vanity, most of us want others to recognize and applaud our virtue. Competitiveness and jealousy are as rampant in the realm of spirituality as they are in other spheres of life. Without examining our own minds and hearts, we criticize others, especially those who appear to be "closer to God" than we are. If for some reason another's virtue is praised in public, most of us feel at least a twinge of jealousy. And when it comes to our religious and spiritual leaders, we are quick with our criticism and harsh in our judgments: "This guy is phony," we think. "What a hypocrite she is!" "Can you believe there are people foolish enough to believe in him and follow him?"

At the collective level, too, we compare our religious beliefs and spiritual practices with those of others, usually with the intention of finding fault and establishing the superiority of our path over theirs. In the external world, the damage caused by religious quarrels is unmistakable—history is replete with martyrs, crusades, inquisitions, pogroms, stonings, burnings, and every other imaginable form of violence committed in the name of God.

In the internal world, the damage caused by competing with others and judging their spiritual attainments is less visible, but no less devastating. Jealousy of fellow seekers and the habit of condemning and judging the path they have chosen pollutes our minds, separates us from others, and leads to violence. The antidote is to cultivate an attitude of cheerfulness and positive appreciation for those who appear to be more virtuous than we are. The following is a contemplative practice for this particular principle:

How delightful it is to see others on the path of virtue and righteousness. Any path, earnestly followed, will certainly lead a spiritual seeker to the highest truth. How grateful I am for those spiritually oriented people whose mere presence on this earth transforms the lives of others. They are the true servants of humanity. The virtues of love, compassion, and selflessness radiate from them. Let me appreciate them and learn from them.

One may also pray in the following manner:

May I constantly remember, "God can verily be worshipped only by those who are more humble and tender than a blade of grass. God can verily be worshipped only by those who have more forbearance and tolerance than the tree that weathers fierce storms and scorching sun in perfect tranquility. God can verily be worshipped only by those who constantly respect all without expecting the slightest respect from others."

Such a contemplative thought, which is a great virtue in itself, can flow spontaneously from our minds and hearts only if we ourselves are cheerful. For without inner cheerfulness, contemplating on the idea of cheerfulness toward others is artificial and becomes a rote mental exercise.

cultivating inner cheerfulness

Cheerfulness is a spontaneous expression of a purified heart and a steady mind. A clear mind is naturally blessed with cheerfulness, and a cheerful person spontaneously loves all and hates none. A cheerful person is fulfilled within, and this cheerfulness overflows, affecting everyone who comes near. On the other hand, an impure mind teems with countless conflicts. Spiritually speaking, a person with such a mind is empty. And one who is empty envies those who are fulfilled, and easily becomes angry and vengeful. Therefore, it is important to cultivate those divine qualities that purify the heart and steady the mind. This will allow cheerfulness to unfold spontaneously.

69

According to *The Bhagavad Gita,* the divine qualities are: fearlessness, steadfastness in knowledge, generosity, self-control, inclination toward studying the revealed scriptures, austerity, non-injury, truthfulness, self-sacrifice, tranquility, compassion, non-possessiveness, modesty, inner strength, forgiveness, fortitude, and absence of hatred and conceit. Unfolding these qualities transforms a human being into a divine being.

The *Gita* also mentions numerous degrading qualities—egoism, ostentation, arrogance, conceit, anger, and rudeness. These are opposed to the divine qualities. They entangle human beings in the web of insatiable desire, hypocrisy, arrogance, lust, anger, and strife and blind them to the knowledge that lust, anger, and greed are the three gates that lead to perdition.

The *Gita* explains how to close these three gates and seal them permanently. This is done by systematically attenuating the degrading qualities and allowing the divine qualities to unfold in their stead. It explains that every activity—physical, verbal, and mental—has three aspects: divine, intermediate, and demonic. By involving ourselves in activities that are intrinsically divine, we move closer to the Divine; the same is true of intermediate and demonic activities.

These three aspects permeate every sphere of action and have a profound influence on what we become. Thus, we can transform ourselves by becoming aware of how these aspects play out in our daily activities. And once we are aware, we can begin to choose to drop the activities that have a demonic influence and engage in those that are divine.

This notion may seem alien to the habitual way most of us have come to regard the world. But a glance at the three aspects at play in a few of our activities will serve to clarify this concept and show how it can be used as a tool of transformation.

F o o d . Divine food is fresh, vibrant, easy to digest, lightly seasoned, cooked by someone who is serene, and earned without hurting others. Such food is pleasing to both our minds and our senses while it is being eaten and while it is being digested. Food which is nutritious but not fresh, and food which is mass-produced, or canned, or whose sole attractive features are appearance and taste, is intermediate food. Demonic food is old, smelly, devoid of nutrients, and painful to the sense of taste, smell, and sight. It is hard to digest and is injurious to our health.

W o r s h i p . Worship dedicated to God, selflessly, lovingly, and without demand or condition is divine worship. Worship dedicated to God or to other forces with the intention of securing a reward—such as power, fame, or material prosperity—is intermediate worship. Demonic worship is dedicated to ghosts and spirits.

A u s t e r i t y . The highest austerity is performed with the single-minded will toward self-discipline, self-discovery, and self-purification. There is no thought of external recognition or reward, because the practice is its own reward. The intermediate type of austerity is performed to demonstrate our virtue to others or to secure a higher post in a religious order. Demonic austerity is undertaken without joy or is imposed by external authority. Any practice of austerity which is a form of torture for the body or the mind is demonic.

C h a r i t y . A charitable act by a generous person who desires nothing in return, directed to the appropriate people at the perfect time, is the highest charity. Altruism and non-attachment to the result are the hallmarks of divine charity. Divine charity is a recognition of our oneness with others. But an act of charity performed with a motive, such as a desire to appear generous, is of the intermediate kind, even when it is enormously beneficial to the recipient. When an act of charity is coerced, or performed out of fear or under social or religious pressure, the act is painful and the memory of this painful act lingers in the mind. This kind of charity is demonic.

71

D i s c i p l i n e . There are three realms of discipline—physical, mental, and verbal. Serving others, cultivating a healthy body, and exercising control over the senses are examples of physical discipline. Cultivating serenity of mind and mental silence, practicing inner control, and striving for purity of heart are forms of mental discipline. Speaking less, voicing only that which is true and sweet, and studying spiritual texts are verbal disciplines.

These disciplines are divine when they are firmly grounded in self-knowledge and when we undertake them joyfully. If we undertake them without understanding why we are doing them or out of a sense of obligation, they are of an intermediate grade. And when these practices are forced on us by parents, teachers, religious institutions, or society, they become a form of torture, not a means of discipline. Thus, they lose their virtue and pull us toward the demonic.

The *Gita* contains similar descriptions of the effect of the three aspects on study, meditation, selfless service, and other spheres of action. The point is that by analyzing our physical, verbal, and mental activities in every area of life, we can transform ourselves and unfold our divine qualities. This is the work of a lifetime. It takes determination, courage, and the willingness to examine all of our habits and to consciously choose those that purify the mind and strengthen the will.

According to yoga, one who cultivates transparency of mind, clarity of thought, and firmness of will becomes light and cheerful. The more cheerful we are, the more difficult it is for painful thoughts to enter our minds. Painful thoughts create fear, insecurity, and delusion. And the less we have of these, the fewer negative feelings we will have for others. A mind unencumbered by negativity is open and spontaneous. Such a mind is clear and is quick to understand. The person possessing such a mind acknowledges and appreciates the virtues of others and is indifferent toward those who seem to be doing evil.

four
indifference toward the non-virtuous

We each have our own definition of "virtue," and if someone is "non-virtuous" according to our definition, the judgmental part of our personality immediately comes forward and we label that person "bad." This colors our thought, speech, and action toward that person. We try to maintain a distance, either by withdrawing ourselves or by pushing them away from us. Or, we try to force them to change. Any of these actions sets the stage for violence.

Again, the only way to change this pattern is to change our own attitudes. We must realize that those whom we consider to be reprehensible or wicked are living according to their own level of understanding. Trying to correct them by criticizing their way of life and values is counterproductive. According to yoga, if it is possible to model the higher values of love, compassion, selflessness, and non-possessiveness for the "non-virtuous," then that should be done. Often a glimpse of the higher virtues is enough to cause a person to reevaluate his or her behavior and to find a way to begin the process of self-transformation.

If we have not acquired the skill of leading someone who we believe to be non-virtuous gently in the direction of self-transformation, the only other option is to cultivate an attitude of indifference—not for the doer but for the deeds. Developing an attitude of indifference toward those who we believe to be non-virtuous damages our sensitivity to others and destroys our capacity for forgiveness, kindness, and selfless love. By cultivating indifference toward the deeds themselves, we remain free of hostility while sending forth the positive energy of love and friendliness.

This attitude of indifference is an act of nonviolence. In developing this attitude, we remain free of animosity for so-called non-virtuous people. We allow them their rightful place, and by refusing to associate the person with the deed, we avoid disturbing ourselves by becoming smug and punitive. By overlooking the lapses of others, we prevent the self-righteousness and discord that leads to violence and war.

73

The following contemplation is helpful in cultivating this attitude:

Let me not heed the actions of those who seem to be wicked or less righteous than me and who are those like me.

Who am I to judge others? How often have I made the mistakes and done that which is not to be done?

Even the most virtuous among us occasionally becomes involved in unworthy deeds or dishonorable behavior. Such things are common to human beings. Let me restrain my mind from dwelling on the apparent frailties of others. My goal is to remain tranquil and loving in the face of all actions.

THE END OF WAR

Practicing these four principles will purify the mind and heart. And once we have developed friendship for those who are happy, compassion for those who are unhappy, cheerfulness toward those who are virtuous, and indifference to non-virtuous acts, we will no longer pose a threat to others, and they will be neither defensive nor self-protective in our presence.

Pure love, compassion, selflessness, and self-acceptance radiate from us when we have purified our hearts. Because similar attracts similar, our presence will elicit these same qualities from others. And so love, compassion, cheerfulness, selflessness, and self-acceptance will begin to radiate from the individual and affect the community, the society, and finally the world. War will no longer be possible—there will be nothing to fight about.

Imagine what a transformation will be wrought in the world when we have transformed ourselves. These four principles are so simple, yet so powerful. When we make them part of ourselves, we'll see only God when we look at others. We will become so open to those around us that we will become their souls and they ours. This is the state called "enlightenment."

According to the scriptures, enlightenment is not something that one achieves from the outside; it is a spontaneous expression of the soul which unfolds when impurities are removed. Those who are enlightened may appear to live in the world and to walk among us, but in truth, they are living in God and walking in the kingdom of God. Because they are living in God, love is the only means they have of sharing their inner wealth.

So let us enlighten ourselves. Let us imbue ourselves with these four virtues and join the company of those whose wisdom is unsurpassed. Again and again the scriptures say that compassion and wisdom go hand in hand. The more compassion we have, the more wisdom we gain; perfection in wisdom is the ground for perfection in compassion. And perfection in compassion is the heart of nonviolence. We can achieve our genuine state of humanness by becoming wise, compassionate, loving, and nonviolent. And only when we become fully human will we truly understand what the scriptures mean when they say, "God created humans in His own image."

Peace, Peace, Peace.

All things are made of one essence, yet things are different according to the forms which they assume under different impressions. As they form themselves so they act, and as they act so they are.

It is as if a potter made different vessels out of the same clay. Some of these pots are to contain sugar, others rice, others curds and milk; others still are vessels of impurity. There is no diversity in the clay used; the diversity of the pots is only due to the molding hands of the potter who shapes them for the various uses that circumstances may require.

And as all things originate from one essence, so they are developing according to one law and they are destined to one aim which is Nirvana. Nirvana comes to you when you understand thoroughly, and when you live according to the understanding that all things are of one essence and there is but one law. Hence, there is but one Nirvana as there is but one truth, not two or three.
—The Gospel of Buddha

May there be harmony in our minds.
May there be harmony in our hearts.
May our perceptions be clear and peaceful.
May we be an ornament to mankind.
—Rig Veda

Out beyond ideas of wrongdoing and rightdoing,
there is a field. I'll meet you there.

When the soul lies down in that grass,
the world is too full to talk about.
Ideas, language, even the phrase "each other"
Doesn't make any sense.
—Rumi

Wars begin in the minds of men, and in those minds,
love and compassion would have built the defenses of peace.
—U Thant

We are what our thoughts have made us; so take care about what
you think. Words are secondary. Thoughts live; they travel far.
—Swami Vivekananda

When you find peace within yourself, you become the
kind of person who can live at peace with others.
—Peace Pilgrim

He who expects to change the world will be disappointed; he must change his view. When this is done, then tolerance will come, forgiveness will come, and there will be nothing he cannot bear.
—Hazrat Inayat Khan

As human beings, our greatness lies not so much in being able to remake the world—that is the myth of the "atomic age"— as in being able to remake ourselves.
—Mahatma Gandhi

Whomsoever Allah desires to guide,
He expands his heart unto the Surrender;
Whomsoever He desires to lead astray,
He makes his heart narrow, tight.
—Koran

Remain quiet.
Discover the harmony in your own being.
Embrace it.

If you can do this, you will gain everything,
and the world will become healthy again.
If you can't, you will be lost in the shadows forever.
—Hua Hu Ching

Violence is a clumsy tool and an unusable one,
and that is why the spirit always lags behind it,
the spirit which knows nothing of force,
whose quests are won by the power of invincible gentleness.
—Rainer Maria Rilke

Concepts create idols; only wonder comprehends anything.
People kill one another over idols.
Wonder makes us fall to our knees.
—Saint Gregory of Nyssa

When the inward and the outward are illuminated,
and all is clear, you are one with the light of sun and moon.
When developed to its ultimate state,
there is a round luminosity which nothing can deceive.
—Liu I Min

When we look into our own hearts and begin to discover
what is confused and what is brilliant, what is bitter and what
is sweet, it isn't just ourselves that we are discovering.
We're discovering the universe. When we discover the Buddha
that we are, we realize that everything and everyone is Buddha.
—Pema Chodron

*Peace comes within the souls of men when they realize their
relationship, their oneness, with the Universe and all its powers,
and when they realize that at the center of the Universe dwells
Waken Tanka [the Great Spirit] and that this center
is really everywhere, it is within each of us.*
—Black Elk

*If three hundred and thirty-three billion Christs appear in the
world, it will do no good unless you yourself undertake to remove
the darkness within. Depend not on others. All these processes
of joining this church or that church, this society or that society,
worshipping this Christ or that Krishna, this fetish or that,
will avail nothing. The only remedy is Light,
and Light is living knowledge, living faith in your Divinity.
That is the remedy. There is no other.*
—Swami Rama Tirtha

*In all four directions God is pervading;
In all four directions He makes merry.
His light spontaneously illuminates—
He is so beautiful!
He is ever-present in all beings.
God destroys the pain of birth and death.
He is the embodiment of mercy.
God is part and parcel of all:
His grandeur will never vanish.*
—Siri Guru Granth Sahib

How did the rose ever open its heart
And give to this world all its beauty?
It felt the encouragement of light against its Being.
Otherwise, we all remain too frightened.

—Hafiz

A human being is part of the whole, called by us "universe,"
a part limited in time and space. He experiences himself,
his thoughts and feelings, as something separate from the rest—
a kind of optical delusion of consciousness. This delusion is
a kind of prison for us, restricting us to our personal desires and
to affection for a few people nearest to us. Our task must be to free
ourselves from this prison by widening our circle of compassion to
embrace all living creatures and the whole of nature in its beauty.

—Albert Einstein

All that is, from the biggest stars to the tiniest speck of dust,
is pervaded by Truth. But the face of Truth is hidden by the
golden disc of worldly charms and temptations. Oh Nourisher
and Eternal Guide of my Life, lift this veil so that
I can see the Truth in its full glory.

—Isha Upanishad

At peace while sitting, at peace while standing . . .
When this state is recognized then one has gone beyond fear.
The one Lord is our protector. He is the guide of every heart.

—Siri Guru Granth Sahib

May we meet in harmony.
Transcending differences,
May we talk in harmony.
May we share what we know.
May we respect what we feel.
By following the path of the Sages,
May we find our rightful place,
And share the wealth granted us.

—Rig Veda

The Lord is the one light shining forth from every creature.
Seeing him present in all, the wise man is humble,
puts not himself forward. His delight is in the Self,
his joy is in the Self, he serves the Lord in all.
Such as he, indeed, are the true knowers of Brahman.

—Mundaka Upanishad

Removing differences and moving from diversity to unity are
the essence of real spiritual practice. This process has to occur at
every level of our individual and social lives. By realizing one
reality within all, we will be able to purify our hearts and minds.
This purification can lead us to the experience of the divine light
within. Once we experience this inner truth, we will find
ourselves to be a part of the universe, and the universe a part of us.

—Swami Rama

I have become what before time I was.
A secret touch has quieted thought and sense:
All things by the agent mind created pass
Into a void and mute magnificence.

—Sri Aurobindo

Everybody today seems to be in such a terrible rush, anxious
for greater developments and greater riches and so on, so that
children have very little time for their parents. Parents have
very little time for each other, and in the home begins the
disruption of the peace of the world.

—Mother Teresa

"He abused me, he beat me, he defeated me, he robbed me,"
—in those who harbor such thoughts hatred will never cease.
"He abused me, he beat me, he defeated me, he robbed me,"
—in those who do not harbor such thoughts hatred will cease.
For never does hatred cease by hatred here below;
hatred ceases by love; this is an eternal law.

—*Dhammapada*

He who says, "I cannot tolerate," shows his smallness;
he who says, "I cannot endure," shows his weakness; he who says,
"I cannot associate," shows his limitation; he who says,
"I cannot forgive," shows his imperfection.

—Hazrat Inayat Khan

You have heard that it was said,
"An eye for an eye and a tooth for a tooth."
But I say to you, Do not resist one who is evil.
But if any one strikes you on the right cheek,
turn to him the other also;
And if any one would sue you and take your coat,
let him have your cloak as well;
And if any one forces you to go one mile,
go with him two miles.
Give to him who begs from you,
and do not refuse him who would borrow from you.
You have heard that it was said,
"You shall love your neighbor and hate your enemy."
But I say to you, Love your enemies
and pray for those who persecute you,
So that you may be sons of your Father who is in heaven;
For he makes his sun rise on the evil and on the good,
and sends rain on the just and on the unjust.
—*Gospel According to Matthew*

I have learned a new form of service from the wars of Frederick,
king of Prussia. It is not necessary to approach the enemy in order
to attack him. In fleeing from him, it is possible to circumvent him
as he advances, and fall on him from the rear until he is forced to
surrender. What is needed is not to strike straight at Evil but to
withdraw to the sources of divine power, and from there to circle
around Evil, bend it, and transform it into its opposite.
—Rabbi Abraham

*One should forgive under any injury. It has been said that the
continuation of the species is due to man being forgiving.
Forgiveness is holiness; by forgiveness the universe is held
together. Forgiveness is the might of the mighty;
forgiveness is sacrifice; forgiveness is quiet of mind.*
—*Mahabharata*

*If you pardon and overlook and forgive,
then surely God is Forgiving, Merciful.*
—*Koran*

*Pay no attention to harsh words uttered by others.
Do not be concerned with what others have or have not done.
Observe your own actions and inactions.*
—*Dhammapada*

*Do not hate one another and do not be jealous of one another and
do not boycott one another, and be servants of God as brethren.*
—*Hadith of Bukhari*

*Judge not, that you be not judged.
For with the judgement you pronounce you will be judged,
and the measure you give will be the measure you get.
Why do you see the speck that is in your brother's eye,
but do not notice the log that is in your own?*
—*Gospel According to Matthew*

Injustice anywhere is a threat to justice everywhere.
We are caught in an inescapable network of mutuality,
tied in a single garment of destiny.
Whatever affects one directly, affects all indirectly.
—Martin Luther King, Jr.

I believe that if one man gains spiritually the whole world
gains with him and, if one man falls, the whole world falls
to that extent. I do not help opponents without at the same time
helping myself and my co-workers.
—*Mahatma Gandhi*

This we know: the Earth does not belong to man, man belongs
to the Earth. All things are connected like the blood that unites
us all. Man did not weave the web of life, he is merely a strand
in it. Whatever he does to the web, he does to himself. As we are
part of the land, you too are part of the land. This Earth is
precious to us. It is also precious to you. One thing we know.
There is only one God. No man, be he Red Man or White Man,
can be apart. We are brothers after all.
—Chief Seattle

When you walk across the fields with your mind pure and holy,
then from all the stones, and all growing things, and all animals,
the sparks of their soul come out and cling to you, and then they
are purified and become a holy fire in you.
—*Hasidic saying*

Protect us together. Nourish us together.
Make us prosperous and vibrant.
May the knowledge of the sages enlighten our lives.
May we always love one another.
Peace, Peace, Peace.
—Upanishads

The experience of love is either a necessity or a luxury. If it be
a luxury, it is expendable; if it be a necessity, then to deny it
is to perish. So simple is the reality, and so terrifying. Ultimately
there is only one place of refuge on this planet for any person—
that is another person's heart. To love is to make of
one's heart a swinging door.
—Howard Thurman

Nonviolence is the answer to the crucial political and moral
questions of our time: the need for man to overcome oppression
and violence without resorting to oppression and violence.
Man must evolve for all human conflict a method which
rejects revenge, aggression and retaliation.
The foundation of such a method is love.
—Martin Luther King, Jr.

Love begets love.
—St. Teresa of Avila

Hatred never ceases by hatred
but by love alone is healed.
This is the ancient and eternal law.

Like a caring mother
holding and guarding the life
of her only child,
so with a boundless heart
hold yourself and all beings.
—Buddha

Effortlessly,
Love flows from God into man,
Like a bird
Who rivers the air
Without moving her wings.
Thus we move in His world
One in body and soul,
Though outwardly separate in form.
As the Source strikes the note,
Humanity sings—
The Holy Spirit is our harpist,
And all strings
Which are touched in Love
Must sound.
—Mechthild of Magdeburg

Hear, O Humankind, the prayer of my heart.

For are we not one, have we not one desire,
to heal our Mother Earth and bind her wounds
to hear again from dark forests and flashing rivers
the varied ever changing Song of Creation?
O humankind, are we not all brothers and sisters,
are we not the grandchildren of the Great Mystery?
Do we not all want to love and be loved, to work
and to play, to sing and dance together?

But we live with fear. Fear that is hate, fear
that is mistrust, envy, greed, vanity, fear that is
ambition, competition, aggression, fear that is
loneliness, anger, bitterness, cruelty... and yet,
fear is only twisted love, love turned back on itself,
love that was denied, love that was rejected.

And love...
Love is life—creation, seed and leaf
and blossom and fruit and seed, love is growth
and search and reach and touch and feed and pleasure,
love is pleasuring ourselves, pleasuring each other,
love is believing in itself.

And life...
Life is the Sacred Mystery singing to itself, dancing
to its drum, telling tales, improvising, playing
and we are all that Spirit, our stories all
but one cosmic story that we are love indeed.

That perfect love in me seeks the love in you,
and if our eyes could ever meet without fear
we would recognize each other and rejoice,
for love is believing in itself.
—Manitongquat

God says to man, as he said to Moses: "Put off thy shoes from
thy feet"—put off the habitual which encloses your foot, and
you will know that the place on which you are now standing is
holy ground. For there is no rung of human life on which we
cannot find the holiness of God everywhere and at all times.
—The Rabbi of Kobryn

"You shall love the Lord your God with all
your heart, and with all your soul, and with all your mind."

This is the great and foremost commandment.
And the second is like it,
"You shall love your neighbor as yourself."
—*Gospel According to Matthew*

Try to treat with equal love all the people with whom you have
relations. Thus the abyss between "myself" and "yourself"
will be filled in, which is the goal of all religious worship.
—Anandamayi Ma

We are called to play the Good Samaritan on life's roadside,
but that will be only an initial act.
One day the whole Jericho road must be transformed
so that men and women will not be beaten and robbed
as they make their journey through life. True compassion
is more than flinging a coin to a beggar;
it understands that an edifice that produces
beggars needs restructuring.
—Martin Luther King, Jr.

Hatred stirs up strife, but love covers all transgressions.
—Proverbs

To be able to love one another, we must pray much, for prayer
gives a clean heart and a clean heart can see God in our neighbor.
If now we have no peace, it is because we have forgotten how to
see God in one another. If each person saw God in his neighbor,
do you think we would need guns and bombs?
—Mother Teresa

While enjoying the objects of the world, a human being can
keep the mind clean and pure only by attaining freedom from
attachment and aversion, and thereby gaining self-mastery.
Clarity of mind eliminates all pains and miseries. It is only in
the purified mindfield that truth is revealed from the source beyond.
—*Bhagavad Gita*

*No loss by flood and lightning, no destruction of cities and temples
by the hostile forces of nature, has deprived man of so many noble
lives and impulses as those which his intolerance has destroyed.*
—Helen Keller

*Truth resides in every human heart, and one has to search for it
there, and to be guided by truth as one sees it. But no one has a
right to coerce others to act according to his own view of truth.*
—Mahatma Gandhi

*Without desire everything is sufficient.
With seeking myriad things are impoverished.
Plain vegetables can soothe hunger.
A patched robe is enough to cover this bent old body.
Alone I hike with a deer.
Cheerfully I sing with village children.
The stream beneath the cliff cleanses my tears.
The pine on the mountain top lifts my heart.*
—Ryokan

*Blessed are the merciful, for they shall obtain mercy.
Blessed are the pure in heart, for they shall see God.
Blessed are the peacemakers,
for they shall be called children of God.*
—Gospel According to Matthew

Thinking about sense-objects
Will attach you to sense-objects;
Grow attached, and you become addicted;
Thwart your addiction, it turns to anger;
Be angry, and you confuse your mind;
Confuse your mind, you forget the lesson of experience;
Forget experience, you lose discrimination;
Lose discrimination, and you miss life's only purpose.
—Bhagavad Gita

Do not lay up for yourselves treasure on earth,
where moth and rust consume
and where thieves break in and steal:
But lay up for yourselves treasure in heaven,
where neither moth nor rust consume
and where thieves do not break in and steal;
For where your treasure is, there will be your heart also.
—Gospel According to Matthew

May our secret acts nourish the common good.
May we meet in peace and harmony.
May our resolve be strong and thoughtful.
May our talks lead to protection and peace.
Through our actions, may we invoke peace
and honor the Truth that resides in all.
—Rig Veda

For man to raise his sword against man, for man to kill man
is not holy war. True holy war is to praise God and to cut away
the enemies of truth within our own hearts. We must cast out all
that is evil within us, all that opposes God. This is the war that
we must fight... Once we understand what the true weapons
of Islam are, we will never take a life, we will never even see
anyone as separate from ourselves. We will not be able to conceive
of any enmity. We will realize that each and every one of us must
act in accordance with Allah's actions and with the same inner
patience, contentment, trust in God, and praise of God
as shown by the Prophet Mohammed.
—M. R. Muhayiaddeen

A skillful soldier is not violent;
An able fighter does not rage;
A mighty conqueror does not give battle;
A great commander is a humble man.

You may call this pacific virtue;
Or say that it is mastery of men;
Or that it is rising to the measure of God
Or to the stature of the ancients.
—Lao Tzu

My creed of nonviolence is an extremely active force. It has no room
for cowardice or even for weakness. There is hope for a violent man
to be someday nonviolent, but there is none for a coward.
—Mahatma Gandhi

Today the world lives under the law of fear, trembling with
doubts and uncertainty. I have met many leaders but have
not encountered any prophet of the law of love. I have yet to
meet that one who teaches selfless service, sympathy,
and goodwill, and who identifies with the true
happiness of others and the highest good of mankind.
—Swami Rama

Creator of peace, compassionate God,
guide us to a covenant of peace with all of Your creatures,
birds and beasts as well as all humanity
reflecting Your image of compassion and peace.
Give us strength to help sustain Your promised covenant
abolishing blind strife and bloody warfare,
so that they will no longer devastate the earth,
so that discord will no longer tear us asunder.
Then all that is savage and brutal will vanish,
and we shall fear evil no more.
Guard our coming and our going,
now toward waking, now toward sleep,
always within Your tranquil shelter.
Beloved are You, Sovereign of peace
whose embrace encompasses Jerusalem,
the people Israel and all humanity.
—*Siddur Sim Shalom*

May there be peace in heaven,
And peace on earth.
May all the waters know peace,
May all the herbs and plants know peace,
May the great trees of the forest know peace.
May all the forces of the universe know peace.
The immense, transcendent Reality is peace.
May all know peace,
Peace and only peace,
And may that peace come unto me.
Om Peace, Peace, Peace.
—Yajur Veda

And they will hammer their swords into plowshares,
and their spears into pruning hooks.
Nation will not lift up sword against nation.
And never again will they learn war.
—Isaiah

Lead me from the unreal to the real.
Lead me from darkness to light.
Lead me from mortality to immortality.
Peace, Peace, Peace.
—Upanishads

From the Himalayan Institute Press

BOOKS

From Death to Birth: Understanding Karma and Reincarnation
  by Pandit Rajmani Tigunait
The Power of Mantra and the Mystery of Initiation
  by Pandit Rajmani Tigunait
Tantra Unveiled by Pandit Rajmani Tigunait
Meditation and Its Practice by Swami Rama
Path of Fire and Light, Volumes 1 and 2 by Swami Rama
A Practical Guide to Holistic Health by Swami Rama
The Royal Path: Practical Lessons on Yoga by Swami Rama
Science of Breath: A Practical Guide by Swami Rama et al.
Yoga: Mastering the Basics by Sandra Anderson and Rolf Sovik
Meditation Is Boring? Putting Life in Your Spiritual Practice
  by Linda Johnsen
Common Sense About Uncommon Wisdom by Dhruv S. Kaji
Choosing a Path by Swami Rama
Freedom from the Bondage of Karma by Swami Rama
Spirituality: Transformation Within and Without by Swami Rama
Yoga and Psychotherapy: The Evolution of Consciousness
  by Swami Rama et al.

TAPES

Eight Steps to Self-Transformation by Pandit Rajmani Tigunait
Nine Steps to Disarming the Mind by Pandit Rajmani Tigunait
Guided Meditation for Beginners by Swami Rama
Learn to Meditate by Rolf Sovik

Pandit Rajmani Tigunait, Ph.D., the spiritual head of the Himalayan Institute, is the successor of Swami Rama of the Himalayas. Lecturing and teaching worldwide for more than a quarter of a century, he is a regular contributor to *Yoga International* magazine, and the author of eleven books, including his classic work, *At the Eleventh Hour: The Biography of Swami Rama of the Himalayas.*

Pandit Tigunait holds two doctorates: one in Sanskrit from the University of Allahabad in India, and another in Oriental Studies from the University of Pennsylvania. Family tradition gave Pandit Tigunait access to a vast range of spiritual wisdom preserved in both the written and oral traditions. Before meeting his master, Pandit Tigunait studied Sanskrit, the language of the ancient scriptures of India; as well as the languages of the Buddhist, Jaina, and Zorastrian traditions. In 1976, Swami Rama ordained Pandit Tigunait into the 5,000-year-old lineage of the Himalayan masters.

While living with his wife and two children, Pandit Tigunait walks in the footsteps of his master—he writes, teaches, guides and administers the work and mission of the Himalayan Institute, joyfully maintaining his commitment to his spiritual pursuits. He attempts to live according to the teachings of the Himalayan sages: "Live in the world, and yet remain above it; find a balance between the sacred and mundane, and between worldly success and inner fulfillment."

The main building of the Institute headquarters, near Honesdale, Pennsylvania.

Founded in 1971 by Swami Rama, the Himalayan Institute is dedicated to helping people grow physically, mentally, and spiritually by combining the best knowledge of both the East and the West.

Our international headquarters is located on a beautiful 400-acre campus in the rolling hills of the Pocono Mountains of northeastern Pennsylvania. The atmosphere fosters growth, increased inner awareness, and calm. Our grounds provide a wonderfully peaceful and healthy setting for our seminars and extended programs. Students from around the world join us here to attend programs in such diverse areas as hatha yoga, meditation, stress reduction, ayurveda, nutrition, Eastern philosophy, psychology, and other subjects. Whether the programs are for weekend meditation retreats, week-long seminars on spirituality, months-long residential programs, or holistic health services, the intent is to provide an environment of gentle inner progress. We invite you to join with us in the ongoing process of personal growth and development.

The Institute is a nonprofit organization. Your membership in the Institute helps to support its programs. Please call or write for information on becoming a member.

Institute programs share an emphasis on conscious holistic living and personal self-development, including:

- Special weekend or extended seminars to teach skills and techniques for increasing your ability to be healthy and enjoy life
- Meditation retreats and advanced meditation and philosophical instruction
- Vegetarian cooking and nutritional training
- Hatha yoga workshops
- Hatha yoga teachers training
- Residential programs for self-development
- Holistic health services, and Ayurvedic Rejuvenation and Pancha Karma Programs through the Institute's Center for Health and Healing.

A Quarterly Guide to Programs and Other Offerings is free within the USA. To request a copy, or for further information, call 800-822-4547 or 570-253-5551, fax 570-253-9078, email info@HimalayanInstitute.org, write the Himalayan Institute, RR 1 Box 1127, Honesdale, PA 18431-9706 USA, or visit our website at www.HimalayanInstitute.org.

the himalayan institute press

The Himalayan Institute Press has long been regarded as "The Resource for Holistic Living." We publish dozens of titles, as well as audio and video tapes, that offer practical methods for living harmoniously and achieving inner balance. Our approach addresses the whole person—body, mind, and spirit—integrating the latest scientific knowledge with ancient healing and self-development techniques.

As such, we offer a wide array of titles on physical and psychological health and well-being, spiritual growth through meditation and other yogic practices, as well as translations of yogic scriptures.

Our yoga accessories include the Japa Kit for meditation practice, the Neti™ Pot, the ideal tool for sinus and allergy sufferers, and The Breath Pillow,™ a unique tool for learning health-supportive diaphragmatic breathing.

Subscriptions are available to a bimonthly magazine, *Yoga International*, which offers thought-provoking articles on all aspects of meditation and yoga, including yoga's sister science, ayurveda.

For a free catalog call 800-822-4547 or 570-253-5551, email hibooks@HimalayanInstitute.org, fax 570-253-6360, write the Himalayan Institute Press, RR 1 Box 1129, Honesdale, PA 18431-9709, USA, or visit our website at www.HimalayanInstitute.org.